THE ULTIMATE
AIR FRYER
COOKBOOK
FOR BEGINNERS

800 Affordable, Healthy and Easy Air Fryer Recipes for Smart People on a Budget

By

Patricia Weiss

Disclaimer

Please note, the information written in this book, are for educational and entertainment purposes only. Strenuous efforts have been made to provide accurate, up to date and reliable complete information in this book. All recommendations are made without guarantee on the part of the author and publisher. By reading this document, the reader agrees that under no circumstances are we responsible for any losses, direct or indirect, which are incurred as a result of the use of the information contained in this document, including but not limited to errors, omissions or inaccuracies.

Table of Contents

INTRODUCTION
Welcome to Air fryer cookbook

New to Air Fryer? Congratulations and welcome aboard to the world of fast and easy cooking. The Air Fryer is a kitchenware that makes use of Rapid Air Technology or hot air to cook the kind of meals that would traditionally be dunked in a deep fat fryer. It has a mechanical fan that circulates the hot air around the food at high speed, cooking the food and producing a crispy layer via the Maillard effect.

Traditional frying methods induce the Maillard effect by completely submerging foods in hot oil. The air fryer works alternatively by coating the desired food in a thin layer of oil while circulating air heated up to 200°C to confer energy and initiate the reaction. They cook with very hot circulating air and provide a healthier alternative to conventional frying because they use little or no oil.

While Air Fryers technically cook by convection roasting rather than frying, it can still deliver results similar to the real frying. Convection ovens and air fryers are very similar in terms of how they cook food, but air fryers are generally smaller than convection ovens and give off less heat when cooking. Similar results can be achieved by using specialized air crisper trays and putting them in the oven. Air fryers are attractive for their convenience, safety, and health benefits.

Health Benefits of Air Frying Your Foods

Air Fryers produce results similar to deep-frying using a little quantity of the oil needed to deep-fry. When deep-frying, you completely submerge the food in oil and the oil is absorbed by the food. In an Air Fryer, you will make use of a tiny fraction of oil to help crisp and brown the foods. The health benefits of air frying include:

1. **Fast and Energy Efficient:**

The Air Fryer can prepare delicious foods quickly and efficiently. While it can take a while for the oven to heat up, your air fryer will heat up within minutes. Most air-fried meals can be prepared in just minutes! While it takes about 15 to 20 minutes to pre-heat our standard ovens, it takes the Air Fryer about 2 to 3 minutes because the Air Fryer is pretty much compacted. That's a huge savings in time as well as energy. During the summer, your Air Fryer can be pre-heated without heating up your whole kitchen.

The intense heat generated in the Air Fryer cooks foods quickly, about 20% faster than in an oven. It simply means that Air Fryers save more time and energy.

2. **No Pollution:**

Most stoves and gas cookers automatically result in some form of environmental pollution or hazards. Air fryers come equipped with cooling systems that keep the machine free from contamination. The Air Fryer has some mechanism for cooling and filtering the heated air before being released into the air. The air filter also prevents the soggy smell of oil from spreading around the kitchen. You can expect to enjoy fresh kitchen smells before and after cooking with an air fryer!

3. **Easy to Use:**

The Air Fryer is incredibly easy to use. Air-frying is safer and easier than deep-frying. Majority of Air Fryers have different settings for time and temperature. There is need to simply enter both and press start. When deep-frying, it involves heating a large pot of oil on the stovetop and makes use of a deep-frying thermometer to measure the temperature and monitor the heat below the pot to maintain that temperature. It is simply difficult and unsafe because you are dealing with a lot of oil, which can be heavy to move, and very dangerous to handle if it gets too hot.

4. **Clean and Tidy:**

We know you would love keeping your kitchen clean and tidy when cooking and after cooking. Deep fryers often result in a messy kitchen. Because an air fryer uses no oil, there aren't any messy clean-ups. The food cooks inside an enclosed fryer, so there's no risk of spills or splatters anywhere. Clean-up after meal is simple and straightforward, which is especially important for time-crunched moms. The entire system is non-stick, and the fryer basket is dishwasher-safe, which makes clean-up quick, simple and painless.

5. **Safe to use:**

Most models of Air Fryers come equipped with an automatic shutdown feature that switches off the machine when the food is cooked. The air fryer has a variety of safety features that make it safe for even newbies to use. With the auto-shutoff feature, you don't have to worry about forgetting to turn the fryer off. Secondly, there's no oil or open flame, which minimizes the risk of kitchen fires and other mishaps. There's no risk of injury due to oil splatters.

Smart Tips and Tricks for Using Your Air fryer

- You have to preheat your Air Fryer for an average of 3 minutes to get the desired temperature. After placing the ingredients in the basket or cooking pot, you have to ensure that there is enough space for the hot air to pass around.

- When you want to prepare pre-made food, like French fries, set the temperature of your Air Fryer to Lower by 70°C than what's standard, and reduce the cooking time on the timer by half for about 15-20 minutes. Although, the temperature and time measurement sure can vary, depending on the type and size of food you're cooking.

- Make use of a non-stick pan or cooking basket to cook and add a drop of oil on the bottom of the pot. When you want to prepare food with excessive fat, for example chicken drumsticks, you should remove any splattering and/or excess vapor and drain the fat.

- Always shake the basket at about half of the cooking dish to ensure that the meal is evenly browned and cooked through. After cooking fatty foods, clean the fat on the bottom of the ingredients after you've finished cooking your meal.

- You should find time to clean your Air Fryer with hot water and low to medium-hard sponge after every single use of the Air Fryer. Dry the Air Fryer with a paper towel after clean with hot water.

General Tips for Air Frying Your Foods

1. **Preparing to Air-fry:**

Keep the Air Fryer in a suitable position in your kitchen. Place your Air Fryer on a level, heat-resistant countertop and ensure that there are at least 5-inches of space behind the Air Fryer where the exhaust vent is located.

Preheat the Air Fryer before adding your food into the Air Fryer basket. Turn your Air Fryer to the exact temperature that you need and set the timer for about 2 or 3 minutes. When the timer goes off, the Air Fryer has preheated and ready to place your food.

Buy lots of kitchen spray bottles to spraying oil on the food and it is better than drizzling or brushing which allows you to use less oil.

2. **Get the Right Accessories:**

When you start air frying, there is need to invest in some accessories for your new kitchen appliance. Baking dishes or cake pans that are oven-safe are also air fryer-safe as well since they do not come in contact with the heating element. The accessory pan needs to fit inside the air fryer basket.

Make an aluminum foil sling to place the accessory pieces into and out of the air fryer basket. The piece of aluminum foil sling has to be folded into a strip about 2-inches wide by 24-inches long. Carefully place the cake pan or baking dish on the foil and by holding the ends of the foil, it will enable you to lift the pan or dish and lower it into the air fryer basket.

Fold the ends of the piece of aluminum foil into the Air Fryer basket, and then return the basket to your Air Fryer. Once you have finished cooking, carefully remove the pan, unfold and hold onto the ends of the aluminum foil to lift the pan out from the basket of your Air Fryer.

3. **While You Are Air-Frying:**

Add enough water when you are cooking fatty foods. Adding enough water to the drawer underneath the basket when cooking helps to prevent grease from getting too hot and smoking. This should be done especially when cooking bacon, sausage, and burgers.

Make use of toothpicks to hold your foods down. This is because the fan from the Air Fryer usually pick up light foods and blow them around when cooking. Therefore, it is advisable to secure foods like the top slice of bread on a sandwich with toothpicks.

Avoid overcrowding the basket. You may prefer to cook your food at one time, but over-crowding the basket will prevent the foods from crisping and browning evenly. So, it's important to cook some of your foods in batches to avoid over-crowding the basket.

Flip the foods over halfway through the cooking time so that they can brown evenly.

4. Shake the Basket While Cooking:

Shake the basket severally during the cooking process to re-distribute the ingredients and enable them to crisp and brown evenly. If there is more than one layer of ingredients in the basket or many ingredients touch each other such as fries and snacks shaking halfway through the process is necessary for an even result. Fragile food should not be air fried in more than one layer, as shaking will damage it the tender foods.

If you do not shake, the hot air cannot reach the areas where the ingredients touch each other. The food in the basket will be cooked, but some areas will not get crispy. By shaking, your food will become more evenly colored and crispier all over. When you shake the basket, you can also check on the color of the ingredients. Spray the basket with spraying oil to get the food to brown and crisp more. Also, spritz it with olive oil during the cooking process to enable the food to brown more evenly.

5. After You Air-Fry:

It is important to remove the Air Fryer basket from the drawer before turning out foods. Do not invert the basket while the basket is still locked into the Air Fryer drawer, it will lead to dumping of all the rendered fat or excess grease onto your plate along with the food you just air-fried.

Don't empty the juices from the drawer too soon because the drawer collects a lot of juices from the cooked foods and catches any marinades that you pour over the food. The flavorful liquid can be served as a sauce to pour over food if the drippings are not too greasy.

6. Clean the Drawer and The Basket After Every Use:

The drawer of your Air Fryer is very easy to clean and when you leave it unwashed, it will lead to the risk of food contamination and your kitchen won't have a nice smell. So, it's very important to wash and clean the drawer and the basket after preparing your meals.

7. Use the Air Fryer to Dry Itself:

Once you have finished washing the Air Fryer basket and drawer, just pop them back into your Air Fryer and turn it on for about 2 to 3 minutes. Both parts will dry itself better than any drying towel.

8. Re-heating Your Foods in The Air Fryer:

There's no exact time and temperature when re-heating leftovers because leftovers vary so significantly. We recommend re-heating your foods in the Air Fryer at 350°F.

Trouble-shooting Tips

Air fryers are solid little machines, but as with any appliance, things can go wrong. Much of what goes wrong with an air fryer can be traced to human error. Here are some problems that are usually due to user confusion and how to correct them:

1. **Lingering food odors:**

The air fryer needs to be cleaned regularly immediately after each meal to avoid lingering odors. Convection cooking sprays tiny particles of food around more than conventional cooking does.

2. **When your food does not turn out as crispy as expected:**

It is pretty much possible to cook crispy potatoes, snacks, meat, poultry or breaded snacks in your Air Fryer. But other foods, such as vegetables, will never get crispy when prepared in the Air Fryer. If you want to obtain crispy results with food that can be air fried, you have to ensure that you are not over-crowding the Air Fryer basket and make use of a tiny fraction of oil. Always shake the basket severally while cooking to ensure even browning and crispiness.

3. **Difficulty of sliding the outer basket into place:**

This is similar to other smaller kitchen appliances such as food processors, juicers, and mixers, all of the parts of an Air Fryers have to be inserted correctly or the appliance won't fit together. Once the basket won't slide in, reassemble the other parts and ensure that they fit snugly and try again. Carefully lift the basket a little while sliding it to position it correctly again.

4. **The Air Fryer is hot to the touch:**

As with any cooking appliance excepting microwaves, Air Fryers become hot to be touched while in use. Always ensure that your Air Fryer is out of reach to your children while cooking to avoid hurting them.

5. **When there is a white smoke coming from the Air Fryer:**

Whenever there is a white smoke coming out from your Air Fryer, add a little amount of water to the Air Fryer drawer underneath the basket. The white smoke is usually as a result of grease that has drained into the drawer and is burning. Adding some water to the drawer will prevent the smoke from coming out.

6. **When there is a black smoke coming from the Air Fryer:**

Kindly turn off the Air Fryer machine and look up towards the heating element inside the fryer. It may be caused as a result of some foods that might have blown up and attached to the heating element, burning and causing the black smoke.

7. **When the Air Fryer machine won't turn off:**

Some of the modern Air Fryers are designed to have a delay in their shutting down process. Immediately you press the power button off, the fan inside the Air Fryer will continue to blow the hot air out of the unit for about 20 seconds. Desist yourself from pressing button again to avoid complications. Exercise some patient and wait for the Air Fryer to turn off.

Air Fryer Recipes Conversion

1. Converting from Traditional Recipes:

The Air Fryer can be used to cook recipes that have instructions for cooking in the oven. This is as a result of the fact that heat in the air fryer is more intense than a standard oven, reduce the suggested temperature by 25°F – 50°F and reduce the time by roughly 20%. So, a recipe that is meant to be cooked at 400°F for 20 minutes, Air-fry at 370°F for about 16 minutes.

2. Converting from Packaged Foods Instructions:

The same uniform rule applies to prepared foods that you may purchase in a grocery store. If a bag of frozen French fries recommends cooking in the conventional oven at 450°F for about 18 minutes, you can cook that same French fries in your Air Fryer at 400°F and start checking them at about 15 minutes. Always remember to shake the basket once or twice during the cooking process to enable the French fries to crisp and brown evenly.

3. Converting to Different Sized Air-Fryers:

Larger Air Fryers can make it easier, especially when you are cooking for 4 or more people because the Air Fryer baskets in these Air Fryers are larger in size. The larger sized Air Fryers will enable you to cook more food at one time and do not have to cook the food in batches.

Always remember not to over-crowd the Air Fryer basket because it will slow down the overall cooking time and result in foods that are not as crispy and evenly browned. Some larger Air Fryers possesses more power to cook foods slightly faster than smaller, lower wattage Air Fryers.

Air Fryers Buyer's Guide

Most Air Fryers look similar, but they don't have the same functionality or features. Here are some of the things you should be aware of when buying your Air Fryer.

1. **Timer:**

The timer varies but can either be a digital or analog implementation. Since food items cook quickly in air fryers, majority of Air Fryers have timers that can be set up to about 30 minutes. If you budget to cook your food for longer, it would be wise to buy an Air Fryer that can go up to 60 minutes.

The analog dials are easier to use, but they usually have some drawbacks because some timers will keep on ticking when the drawer housing the food is removed. Air Fryer with a digital timer tends to be better and more accurate with time keeping but they also tend to be costlier.

2. **Temperature Setting:**

Different foods require different temperatures to achieve optimal results. Some foods such as pork or bacon will require different temperature settings than cooking potato wedges. Majority of Air Fryers comes with a range of roughly 200°F – 400°F which is plenty of variation to cook a wide variety of food items.

It's worthy of note that if your Air Fryer can't reach a certain temperature that is required for a particular recipe, all you have to do is to cook the food longer. The temperature settings can be implemented either digitally or via an analog display too.

3. **Size and Capacity:**

Air Fryers comprises of a variety of sizes and the capacity is measured in quarts, pounds, or liters. You should buy a smaller unit if you aim to be cooking for one or two people or you are cooking smaller units of food. Larger Air Fryers should be considered for purchase if you want to cook larger quantities of food for more people two people.

4. **Pre-set Cooking Programs:**

The pre-set cooking programs of digital Air Fryers enables you to automatically set the time and temperature by the pushing of a button for a number of common food items. Some Air Fryers have their functional settings printed on their lid or body.

5. **Safety features:**

Most Air Fryers today come with a host of safety features. These safety features include a cool touch handle, a safety button on the handle to prevent the Air Fryer basket from falling when taking out your food, and an automatic shut off ability when the timer expires. Air Fryers are designed to prevent the smoke from building up and also protect the internal components from getting dirty or damaged.

6. **Cleaning:**

The components of the Air Fryers that usually gets dirty such as the bottom drawer and basket are dishwasher safe. This implies that you can throw them in the dishwasher for a good clean. The majority of parts of this home device are removable as well as dishwasher-safe. This which means that you no longer need to use up too much of your time to scrape the pan as well as strive to make sure every little thing is tidy. Some components like a mesh basket or grated grill are prone to food items becoming stuck on them and so it is necessary to clean them in dishwater.

7. **Accessories**

Some accessories like mesh basket, racks and tongs comes along with a newly purchased Air Fryer. These accessories make it easier to have grill racks and pans to help handle other food items more comfortably.

BREAKFAST RECIPES

Breakfast Sausage

Preparation time: 10 minutes

Cooking time: 10 minutes

Overall time: 20 minutes

Serves: 2 to 6 people

Recipe Ingredients:

- ❖ 1 pound of ground pork
- ❖ 1 pound of ground turkey
- ❖ 2 teaspoons of fennel seeds
- ❖ 2 teaspoon of dry rubbed sage
- ❖ 2 teaspoons of garlic powder
- ❖ 1 teaspoon of paprika
- ❖ 1 teaspoon of sea salt
- ❖ 1 teaspoon of dried thyme
- ❖ 1 tablespoon of real maple syrup

Cooking Instructions:

1. In a large bowl, mix-up the pork and turkey. Again, in a small bowl, mix together the remaining ingredients: fennel, sage, garlic powder, paprika, salt, and thyme.

2. Pour spices into the meat and continue to stir until the spices are properly mixed together.

3. Spoon into balls for about 2 to 3 tablespoons of meat, and flatten into patties.

4. Then place inside the air fryer, you will probably have to do this in 2 batches.

5. Set the temperature at 370ºF, and cook for about 10 minutes. Remove from the air fryer and repeat with the remaining sausage.

6. Serve immediately and enjoy.

Hash Brown

Preparation time: 15 minutes

Cooking time: 15 minutes

Total time: 30 minutes

Serves: 2 to 8 people

Recipe Ingredients:

- ❖ 4 peeled and finely grated large potatoes
- ❖ 2 tbsp. of corn flour
- ❖ Salt
- ❖ Pepper powder
- ❖ 2 tsp. of chili flakes
- ❖ 1 tsp. of garlic powder (optional)
- ❖ 1 tsp. of onion powder (optional)
- ❖ 2 tsp. of vegetable oil

Cooking Instructions

- ❖ Soak the shredded potatoes in cold water and drain out the water. Repeat the step to drain excess starch from potatoes.

- ❖ In a non-stick pan, heat 1 teaspoon of vegetable oil and sauté shredded potatoes until it is cooked slightly for 3 to 4 minutes.

- ❖ Cool it down and transfer the potatoes to a plate and add corn flour, salt, pepper, garlic, onion powder and chili flakes.

- ❖ Mix together thoroughly, then spread over the plate and pat it firmly with your fingers.

- ❖ Refrigerate it for 20 minutes. After that preheat Air-fryer at 180°C. Now take out the now refrigerated potato and divide into equal pieces with a knife.

- ❖ Brush the wire basket of the Air-fryer with little oil.

- ❖ Serve immediately and enjoy.

French Toast Sticks

Preparation time: 5 minutes

Cooking time: 12 minutes

Overall time: 17 minutes

Serves: 2 to 4 people

Recipe Ingredients:

- ❖ 4 pieces of bread
- ❖ 2 tablespoons of butter
- ❖ 2 eggs
- ❖ 1 pinch of salt
- ❖ 1 pinch of cinnamon
- ❖ 1 pinch of nutmeg
- ❖ 1 pinch of ground cloves
- ❖ 1 teaspoon of icing sugar

Cooking Instructions:

- ❖ Preheat Air-fryer at 180°C.Then gently beat together two eggs in a bowl, sprinkle salt, a few heavy shakes of cinnamon, small pinches of both nutmeg and ground cloves.

- ❖ Butter both sides of bread slices and cut into strips. Dredge each strip in the egg mixture and arrange in Air-fryer (cook in two batches).

- ❖ After a period of 2 minutes cooking, pause the Air-fryer to take out the pan, making sure you place the pan on a heat safe surface, spraying the bread with cooking spray.

- ❖ Once you have generously coated the strips, flip and spray the second side as well.

- ❖ Return pan to fryer and heat for4 minutes. Check after a couple minutes to ensure they are cooking evenly and not burning.

- ❖ When egg is cooked and bread is golden brown, remove from Air-fryer.

- ❖ Note: to garnish, sprinkle with icing sugar, top with whip cream and drizzle with maple syrup, or serve with a small bowl of syrup for dipping.

- ❖ Serve immediately and enjoy!

Air-fryer Bagels

Preparation time: 5 minutes

Cooking time: 4 minutes

Overall time: 9 minutes

Serves: 2 to 4 people

Recipe Ingredients:

- ❖ 2 bagels (refrigerated /room temperature) opened for toasting

Cooking Instructions:

1. Preheat your Air-fryer at 360°F or 176°C for 5 minutes and add bagels to the air fryer in a single layer.

2. Air-fry your bagels for about4 minutes at 360°F or 176°C.

3. If you have larger bagels, you may to add extra 1 to 2 minutes depending on your toasting preferences.

4. Top with jam, serve and enjoy!

Home-fries /Breakfast Potatoes

Preparation time: 10 minutes

Total time: 25 minutes

Overall time: 35 minutes

Serves: 4 to 6 people

Recipe Ingredients:

- ❖ 2 to 3 large potatoes
- ❖ 1 diced onion
- ❖ 1 red diced pepper
- ❖ 1 tsp. of garlic powder
- ❖ ½ tsp. of paprika
- ❖ 1 tsp. of salt
- ❖ 1 tbsp. of spritz oil

Cooking Instructions:

1. Preheat your Air-fryer at 390° F for about 5 minutes and then in a large bowl, mix together all ingredients.

2. If you use an oil mister, simply mist the mixture until you achieve the desired amount of oil you want. Without additional oil, your potatoes will stick together.

3. Then add a liner to your Air-fryer; otherwise, you can spritz the bottom of the Air-fryer basket to prevent sticking.

4. Place potatoes in the basket of your Air-fryer. Your cooking time will vary by the volume of potatoes you place in your Air-fryer at once.

5. Cook at 390°F for about 15 to 20 minutes, shaking frequently, setting your time for 18 minutes.

6. Serve in a plate and enjoy!

Hard-Boiled Eggs

Preparation time: 10 minutes

Cooking time: 15 minutes

Overall time: 25 minutes

Serves: 4 to 6 people

Recipe Ingredients

- ❖ 6 Large eggs
- ❖ 1 to 2 spritz oil

Cooking Instructions:

1. Place the wire rack or egg attachment that came with your air fryer or accessory kit in the Air-fryer.

2. If you do not have a wire rack, you may place them gently in the bottom, but be aware that the eggs may move around.

3. Place all 6 eggs on the wire rack. If any eggs are touching each other, lightly oil the eggs as they will stick together. Then cook at 260°F for about 15 minutes.

4. After 15 minutes, remove eggs and place them in an ice-water bath immediately for 10 minutes then refrigerate.

5. Peel and enjoy!

Ultimate Cinnamon Toast

Preparation time: 3minutes

Cooking time: 8 minutes

Overall time: 11minutes

Serves: 2 people

Recipe Ingredients:

- ❖ 2 slices of your favorite bread
- ❖ 1 teaspoon of cinnamon
- ❖ 1 teaspoon of brown sugar
- ❖ 1 teaspoon of granulated sugar
- ❖ 1 tablespoon of butter (Softened)

Cooking Instructions:

1. In a small bowl, mix together cinnamon, brown sugar, and granulated sugar and set aside.

2. Preheat your Air-fryer at 400°F for a period of 5 minutes. After, that butter your bread slices uniformly. Butter both sides for twice sugar on your cinnamon toast.

3. Air-fry at 400°F for roughly 3 minutes, or until desired quality is achieved.

4. Sprinkle on your cinnamon and sugar mixture and cover thoroughly.

5. Serve immediately and enjoy!

Air-fryer Bacon

Preparation time: 5 minutes

Cooking time: 15 minutes

Overall time: 20 minutes

Serves: 2 to 4 people

Recipe Ingredients:

- ❖ 4 Slices Bacon (2 slices per serving) depending on the capacity of your Air-fryer.

Cooking Instructions:

1. Preheat your Air-fryer at 350°F for about 5 minutes. A rack will be needed so that your bacon doesn't sit in a pile of bacon grease.

2. Place 4 strips of your favorite bacon in the basket of your Air-fryer.

3. If you have a smaller Air-fryer, you may cut your bacon in half so it fits on the rack and cook at 350°F for about 10 minutes.

4. Serve immediately and Enjoy!

Muffin Quiche

Preparation time: 4 minutes

Cooking time: 12 minutes

Overall time: 16 minutes

Serves: 3 to 9 people

Recipe Ingredients

- ❖ 3 eggs
- ❖ ¼ cup of shredded cheese
- ❖ 2 patties of sausage cooked and crumbled
- ❖ Salt
- ❖ Pepper

Cooking Instructions

1. Crack eggs in a bowl and mix with cheese and sausage crumbles. Add salt and pepper to taste.

2. Pour mixture into silicone muffin cups and place in the air fryer basket and cook at 350°F for about 12 minutes.

3. Plate, serve and enjoy!

Buttermilk Biscuits

Preparation time: 2 minutes

Cooking time: 8 minutes

Over all time: 10 minutes

Serves: 2 to 4 people

Recipe Ingredients

- ❖ 1 can of your favorite buttermilk biscuits.

Cooking Instructions

1. Place a parchment liner in the bottom of your Air-fryer basket, or mist it with oil.

2. Place the biscuits in your Air-fryer basket and bake at 340°F for approximately 8 minutes.

3. Serve immediately and enjoy!

Frozen Sausages

Preparation time: 2 minutes

Cooking time: 10 minutes

Overall time: 12 minutes

Recipe Ingredients:

- ❖ 1 package of your favorite frozen breakfast sausage

Cooking Instructions:

1. Preheat your Air-fryer at 400°F for about 5 minutes, then line the bottom of your Air-fryer basket with a parchment liner.

2. Add Sausage patties to your Air-fryer basket in one layer. The single-layer makes for cooking the sausage squarely.

3. Cook at 400°F for about 5 minutes for smaller sausages and 10 minutes for larger sausages.

4. Your small standard sausage link will take 5 minutes, while your large chicken sausage will take 10 minutes.

5. Determine your sausage type, and adjust time as required.

6. Due to diversities in cook times for sausage links, use a meat thermometer to ensure that your sausage is cooked to 160°F.

7. Serve, and enjoy!

Cinnamon Rolls

Preparation time: 2 minutes

Cook time 15 minutes

Overall time 17 minutes

Recipe Ingredients:

- ❖ 1 can of cinnamon rolls
- ❖ 1 spray of non-stick of cooking spray

Recipe Instructions:

1. Place the cinnamon rolls in the basket of your air fryer, using parchment paper rounds or non-stick cooking spray.

2. Cook at 340°F for about 15 minutes, turning it once.

3. Drizzle with icing, serve immediately and enjoy!

Breakfast-style potatoes

Preparation time: 6 minutes

Cooking time: 25 minutes

Overall time: 31 minutes

Serves: 2 to 4 people

Recipe Ingredients:

- ❖ 2 (13 oz.) medium sized russet potatoes
- ❖ Few generous spritzes oil spray
- ❖ Pinch of salt and pepper
- ❖ 1 small chopped bell pepper (5 oz. - ¾ cup
- ❖ 1 small chopped onion (4 oz. – ¾ cup)

Cooking Instructions:

- ❖ Put potatoes into Air-fryer basket. Spritz with oil spray, shake and spritz again, then add a pinch of salt.

- ❖ Air-fry at 400°F for about 10 minutes. Stop once to shake during cooking time. Stir if the potatoes aren't moving around enough.

- ❖ After the potatoes have cooked for 10 minutes, add the bell pepper and onions.

- ❖ Add another spritz of oil, and shake basket. Then Air-fry at 400°F for more 15 minutes.

- ❖ During the last 5 minutes of cooking, check on the potatoes to make sure they aren't getting too brown.

- ❖ Depending on the size of your potatoes, you may need slightly less or slightly more time. If needed, add a few more minutes to the cooking time.

- ❖ Add salt to taste and serve immediately.

Breakfast Frittata

Preparation time: 5 minutes

Cooking time: 16 minutes

Overall time: 21 minutes

Serves: 4

Recipe Ingredients:

- ❖ 4 Eggs
- ❖ 3 tbsp. of heavy cream double cream
- ❖ 4 tbsp. of grated cheddar cheese
- ❖ 4 mushrooms sliced
- ❖ 3 grape tomatoes cherry tomatoes, halved
- ❖ 4 tbsp. of chopped spinach
- ❖ 2 tbsp. of fresh chopped herbs of choice
- ❖ 1 green onion sliced
- ❖ Salt to taste

Cooking Instructions:

1. Preheat your airfryer at 350°F, line a deep 7-inch baking pan with parchment paper, then oil the pan and set it aside.

2. In a bowl, whisk together the eggs and cream, after that, add the rest of the ingredients to the bowl, and stir thoroughly to combine.

3. Pour the breakfast frittata mixture into the baking pan and place inside the air fryer basket.

4. Cook for about 12 to 16 minutes, or until eggs are set. Note: to check, insert a toothpick in the center of the Air-fryer frittata. The eggs are set if it comes out clean.

5. Serve immediately and enjoy.

Ham and Egg Toast Cups

Preparation time: 5 minutes

Cooking time: 20 minutes

Overall time: 25 minutes

Recipe Ingredients:

- ❖ 4 Ramekins
- ❖ 4 Eggs
- ❖ 8 Slices of toast
- ❖ 2 Slices of Ham
- ❖ Butter
- ❖ Salt
- ❖ Pepper
- ❖ Cheese (if desired)

Cooking Instructions:

1. Firstly, brush the interior of the ramekin with a generous amount of butter with a cooking brush. The more butter, the easier it is to remove the toast cups from the ramekins.

2. Flatten 8 slices of toast with either a rolling pin or your own palm. Make it as flat as possible.

3. Line the inside of each ramekin with a slice of flattened toast. But try to pinch the extra folds and make it as nice a cup as possible.

4. Place another slice of flattened toast on top of the first toast and likewise, try to flatten the extra folds

5. Cut 2 slices of ham into 8 smaller strips and line 2 strips of ham in each ramekin.

6. Crack an egg into each toast cup and add a pinch of salt and some ground black pepper into each egg. You may also add some cheese into the toast cup.

7. Place all 4 ramekins into the Air-fryer for 15 minutes at 160°F. Do not preheat the Air-fryer in advance.

8. Once done, remove the ramekins from the Air-fryer with whatever kitchen contraception you have that protects your fingers from the heat.

9. To remove the toast cup from the ramekins, you can use a small knife and slowly sliced it round the inside of the ramekin just in case some bread got stuck to the sides.

10. Then twist the toast cup out of the ramekin with the same small knife and a spoon.

11. When done serve and enjoy!

Breakfast Casserole

Preparation time: 10 minutes

Cooking time: 15 minutes

Overall time: 25 minutes

Serves: 8 people

Recipe Ingredients:

- ❖ 1 pound of ground sausage
- ❖ ¼ cup of diced white onion
- ❖ 1 diced green bell pepper
- ❖ 8 whole eggs, beaten
- ❖ ½ cup of shredded colby jack cheese
- ❖ 1 teaspoon of fennel seed
- ❖ ½ teaspoon of garlic salt

Cooking Instructions:

1. Firstly, add in the onion and pepper and cook along with the ground sausage until the veggies are soft and the sausage is cooked.

2. Making the 8.75-inch pan or the Air-Fryer pan, spray it with non-stick cooking spray.

3. Place the ground sausage mixture on the bottom of the pan and top evenly with cheese.

4. Pour the beaten eggs calmly over the cheese and sausage and add fennel seed and garlic salt evenly over the eggs. Then set to Air Crisp for 15 minutes at 390ºF.

5. Carefully remove and serve immediately!

Wake up Avocado Boats

Preparation time: 10 minutes

Cooking time: 7 minutes

Overall time: 17 minutes

Serves: 1 to 2 people

Recipe Ingredients:

- ❖ 2 avocados, halved and pitted
- ❖ 2 plum tomatoes, seeded and diced
- ❖ ¼ cup of diced red onion
- ❖ 2 tablespoons of chopped fresh cilantro
- ❖ 1 tbsp. finely diced jalapeno (optional)
- ❖ 1 tbsp. of lime juice
- ❖ ½ tsp. of salt
- ❖ ¼ tsp. of black pepper
- ❖ 4 eggs

Cooking Instructions:

1. Using a spoon, scoop the avocado pulp out of the skin, keeping shell intact. Dice avocado and place in a medium bowl.

2. Toss with tomato, onion, cilantro, jalapeno (if desired), lime juice, salt, and pepper. Cover and refrigerate avocado mixture until ready to use.

3. Preheat Air-fryer to 350ºF.To ensure that avocado shells don't rock while cooking, place them on a foil ring.

4. To make them, simply roll two 3-inch-wide strip of aluminum foil into rope shapes and form each one into a 3-inch circle.

5. Place each avocado shell on a foil ring in Air-fryer basket. Break 1 egg into each avocado shell and air-fry for about 5 to 7 minutes or until desired texture is given.

6. Take out from basket; top with avocado salsa, serve and enjoy.

POULTRY RECIPES

Air-fryer Blackened Chicken Breast

Preparation time: 10 minutes

Cooking time: 20 minutes

Extra time: 10 minutes

Overall time: 40 minutes

Serves: 2 to 3 people

Recipe Ingredients:

- ❖ 2 tsp. of paprika
- ❖ 1 tsp. of ground thyme
- ❖ 1 tsp. of cumin
- ❖ ½ tsp. of cayenne pepper
- ❖ ½ tsp. of onion powder
- ❖ ½ tsp. of black pepper
- ❖ ¼ tsp. of salt
- ❖ 2 tsp. of vegetable oil
- ❖ 2 (12 ounce) of skinless, boneless chicken breast halves

Cooking Instructions:

1. Mix up paprika, thyme, cumin, cayenne pepper, onion powder, black pepper, and salt thoroughly in a bowl, then transfer spice mixture to a flat plate.

2. Rub oil over each chicken breast until fully coated. Roll each piece of chicken in blackening spice mixture and making sure its press down so that spice sticks on all sides.

3. Let it sit for about 5 minutes while you preheat the air-fryer at 360ºF for 5 minutes.

4. Place chicken in the basket of the Air-fryer and cook for 10 minutes. Flip and cook an additional 10 minutes.

5. Then transfer chicken to a plate and let it rest for 5 minutes. Serve and enjoy!

Chicken Thigh Schnitzel

Preparation time: 15 minutes

Cooking time: 10 minutes

Overall time: 25 minutes

Serves: 2 to 4 people

Recipe Ingredients:

- ❖ 1-pound skinless, boneless chicken thighs, trimmed of fat
- ❖ ½ cup of seasoned bread crumbs
- ❖ 1 teaspoon of salt
- ❖ ½ teaspoon of ground black pepper
- ❖ ¼ cup of flour
- ❖ 1 egg, beaten
- ❖ 1 avocado oil cooking spray

Cooking Instructions:

1. Place your chicken thighs, 1 at a time, between 2 sheets of parchment paper and flatten it with a mallet.

2. Combine your bread crumbs, salt, and black pepper in a shallow bowl thoroughly.

3. Place your flour in a separate shallow bowl and beaten egg in a third shallow bowl.

4. Dip chicken thighs first in flour, then in beaten egg, and finally, coat with bread crumb mixture.

5. Preheat your Air-fryer at 375°F. After that, place breaded thighs in the air fryer basket, making sure they are not touching; work in batches if necessary.

6. Mist with avocado oil and cook for 6 minutes. Flip each thigh, mist with oil, and cook an additional 3 to 4 minutes.

7. Serve and enjoy!

Sesame Chicken Thighs

Preparation time: 5 minutes

Cooking time: 15 minutes

Extra time: 35 minutes

Overall time: 55 minutes

Serves: 4 to 6 people

Recipe Ingredients:

- 2 tbsp. of sesame oil
- 2 tbsp. of soy sauce
- 1 tbsp. of honey
- 1 tbsp. of sriracha sauce
- 1 tsp. of rice vinegar
- 2 lb. of chicken thighs
- 1 green onion, chopped
- 2 tbsp. of toasted sesame seeds

Cooking Instructions:

1. Mix-up sesame oil, soy sauce, honey, sriracha, and vinegar in a large bowl.

2. Add chicken and stir thoroughly to combine. Cover and refrigerate for about 30 minutes.

3. Preheat your air fryer at 400ºF while draining marinade from the chicken.

4. Place chicken thighs skin-side up in the basket of the air fryer and Cook for 5 minutes. After 5 minutes, flip and cook an additional 10 minutes.

5. Transfer chicken to a plate and let it rest for 5 minutes before serving. Garnish with green onion and sesame seeds.

6. Serve and enjoy!

BBQ Cheddar-Stuffed Chicken Breasts

Preparation: 10 minutes

Cooking time: 22 minutes

Overall time: 32 minutes

Serves: 2 to 4 people

Recipe Ingredients:

- 3 strips of bacon, divided
- 2 oz. of cheddar cheese, cubed, divided
- ¼ cup of barbeque sauce, divided
- 2 (4 oz.) of skinless, boneless chicken breasts
- 1 pinch of salt and ground black pepper to taste

Cooking Instructions:

1. Preheat your air fryer at 380°F. After that, cook 1 strip of bacon in the Air-fryer for about 2 minutes.

2. Remove from air fryer and cut into small pieces. Line the air fryer basket with parchment paper and increase the temperature to 400°F.

3. Mix-up cooked bacon, cheddar cheese, and 1 tablespoon of barbeque sauce in a bowl thoroughly.

4. Use a long, sharp knife to make a horizontal 1-inch cut at the top of each chicken breast, creating a small internal pouch.

5. Stuff each breast equally with bacon-cheese mixture. Wrap remaining strips of bacon around each chicken breast.

6. Coat chicken breast with remaining barbecue sauce and place into the prepared Air-fryer basket.

7. Cook for 10 minutes in the Air-fryer, turn, and continue cooking until chicken is no longer pink in the center and the juices run clear for about 10 minutes more.

8. Use a meat thermometer to ensure that the centre has reached an internal temperature of 165°F for medium well. Serve and enjoy!

Mexican-Style Air-fryer Stuffed Chicken Breasts

Preparation: 20 minutes

Cooking time: 11 minutes

Overall time: 31 minutes

Serves: 2 people

Recipe Ingredients:

- ❖ 4 eaches extra-long toothpicks
- ❖ 4 tsp. of chili powder, divided
- ❖ 4 tsp. of ground cumin, divided
- ❖ 1 skinless, boneless chicken breast
- ❖ 2 tsp. of chipotle flakes
- ❖ 2 tsp. of Mexican oregano
- ❖ 1 pinch of salt and ground black pepper to taste
- ❖ ½ red bell pepper, sliced into thin strips
- ❖ ½ onion, sliced into thin strips
- ❖ 1 fresh of jalapeno pepper, sliced into thin strips
- ❖ 2 tsp. of corn oil
- ❖ ½ lime juiced

Recipe Instructions:

1. Place toothpicks in a small bowl and cover with water; let them soak to keep them from burning while cooking.

2. Mix 2 teaspoons of chili powder and 2 teaspoons of cumin in a shallow dish.

3. Preheat your Air-fryer at 400°F. After preheating, place your chicken breast on a flat work surface.

4. Slice horizontally through the middle. Pound each half using a kitchen mallet or rolling pin until about 1/4-inch thick.

5. Sprinkle each breasts half equally with remaining chili powder, remaining cumin, chipotle flakes, oregano, salt, and pepper.

6. Place ½ the bell pepper, onion, and jalapeno in the center of 1 breast half. Turn the chicken from the tapered end upward and use 2 toothpicks to secure.

7. Repeat with other breast, spices, and vegetables and secure with remaining toothpicks.

8. Turn each roll-up in the chili-cumin mixture in the shallow dish while drizzling with olive oil until evenly covered.

9. Position roll-ups in the air-fryer basket with the toothpick side facing up and set timer for 6 minutes.

10. Turn roll-ups over. Continue cooking in the air fryer until juices run clear.

11. Use instant-read thermometer inserted into the center to ensure the internal temperature has reached 165ºF for about 5 minutes more.

12. Drizzle lime juice uniformly on roll-ups before serving.

Buffalo Chicken

Preparation time: 20 minutes

Cooking time: 8 minutes

Overall time: 28 minutes

Serves: 4 to 6 people

Recipe Ingredients:

- ½ cup of plain fat-free greek yogurt
- ¼ cup of egg substitute
- 1 tbsp. of hot sauce
- 1 tsp. hot sauce
- 1 cup of panko bread crumbs
- 1 tbsp. of sweet paprika
- 1 tbsp. of garlic pepper seasoning
- 1 tbsp. of cayenne pepper
- 1 lb. of skinless, boneless chicken breasts, cut into 1-inch strips

Recipe Instructions:

1. Whisk Greek yogurt, egg substitute, and 1 tablespoon plus 1 teaspoon hot sauce in a bowl thoroughly.

2. Mix panko bread crumbs, paprika, garlic pepper, and cayenne pepper in a separate bowl.

3. Dip chicken strips into yogurt mixture; coat with panko bread crumb mixture. After mixture, arrange coated chicken strips in a single layer in an air fryer.

4. Cook until it's uniformly browned for about 8 minutes per side.

5. Serve immediately and enjoy!

Crispy Ranch Air-Fryer Nuggets

Preparation time: 15 minutes

Cooking time: 10 minutes

Extra time: 15 minutes

Overall: 40 minutes

Serves: 4 to 6 people

Recipe Ingredients:

- 1 lb. of chicken tenders, cut into 1.5 to 2-inch pieces
- 1 (1 oz.) package of dry ranch salad dressing mix
- 2 tbsp. offlour
- 1 egg, lightly beaten
- 1 cup of panko bread crumbs
- 1 serving olive oil cooking spray

Cooking Instructions:

1. Place chicken in a bowl, sprinkle with ranch seasoning, and toss to combine. Let it sit for about 5 to 10 minutes.

2. Place flour in a re-sealable bag. Place egg in a small bowl and panko bread crumbs on a plate.

3. Preheat air fryer to 390ºF, then place chicken into the bag and toss to coat. Lightly dip chicken into egg mixture, letting excess drip off.

4. Roll chicken pieces in panko, pressing crumbs into the chicken. Spray basket of the Air-fryer with oil and place chicken pieces inside, making sure it does not overlap.

5. You may have to do two batches, depending on the size of your air fryer. Lightly mist chicken with cooking spray and cook for 4 minutes.

6. Turn chicken pieces and cook until chicken it's no longer pink on the inside, about 4 more minutes. Serve immediately and enjoy.

Honey-Cajun Chicken Thighs

Preparation: 10 minutes

Cooking time: 25 minutes

Extra time: 30 minutes

Overall time: 1 hr 5 minutes

Serves: 4 to 6 people

Recipe Ingredients:

- ½ cup of buttermilk
- 1 tsp. of hot sauce
- 1 ½ lb. of skinless, boneless chicken thighs
- ¼ cup of all-purpose flour
- ⅓ cup of tapioca flour
- 2 ½ tsp. of Cajun seasoning
- ½ tsp. of garlic salt
- ½ tsp. of honey powder
- ¼ tsp. of ground paprika
- ⅛ tsp. of cayenne pepper
- 4 tsp. of honey

Cooking Instructions:

1. Combine buttermilk and hot sauce in a re-sealable plastic bag. Add chicken thighs and marinate for 30 minutes.

2. Combine flour, tapioca flour, Cajun seasoning, garlic salt, honey powder, paprika, and cayenne pepper in a small bowl thoroughly.

3. Remove thighs from buttermilk mixture and dredge through flour mixture and shake off excess flour.

4. Preheat your Air-fryer at 360°Fand place chicken thighs into the Air-fryer basket and cook for about 15 minutes.

5. Flip thighs over and cook until chicken thighs are no longer pink in the center and the juices run clear for about 10 more minutes.

6. Use a meat thermometer to ensure that the center has reached an internal temperature of 165ºF.

7. Remove chicken thighs from air fryer and drizzle each thigh with 1 teaspoon of honey.

8. Serve and enjoy!

Bacon-Wrapped Chicken Thighs

Preparation: 10 minutes
Cooking time: 25 minutes
Extra time: 2 hrs
Overall time: 2 hrs 35 minutes
Serves: 4 to 8 people

Recipe ingredients:

- ½ stick butter, softened
- ½ clove minced garlic
- ¼ tsp. of dried thyme
- ¼ tsp. of dried basil
- ⅛ tsp. of coarse salt
- 1 pinch of freshly ground black pepper
- ⅓ lb. of thick-cut bacon
- 1 ½ lb. of boneless skinless chicken thighs
- 2 tsp. of minced garlic
- Finishing butter

Cooking Instructions:

1. Combine softened butter, garlic, thyme, basil, salt, and pepper in a bowl and stir.

2. Place butter on a piece of wax paper and roll up rightly to form a butter log. Then refrigerate until it becomes firm for about 2 hours.

3. Lay one bacon strip flat on a piece of wax paper. Place chicken thigh on top of the bacon and sprinkle with garlic.

4. Open up the chicken thigh and place 1 to 2 teaspoons of the cold finishing butter in the middle of the chicken thigh.

5. Push one end of bacon into the middle of the chicken thigh. Fold over the chicken thigh and roll the bacon around the chicken thigh and repeat with remaining thighs and bacon.

6. Preheat your air fryer at 370°F and place chicken thighs in the basket of the   Air-fryer and cook until chicken is no longer pink and the juices run clear for about 25 minutes.

7. An instant-read thermometer put in near the bone should read 165°F to verify readiness. Serve immediately and enjoy!

Whole Turkey with Gravy

Preparation time: 10 minutes

Cooking time: 3 hour 15 minutes

Overall time3 hours 25 minutes

Serves: 6 to 7 people

Recipe Ingredients:

- ❖ 14 pounds of raw whole turkey
- ❖ 6 tbsp. of butter, cut into slices
- ❖ 4 cloves of garlic, sliced thin
- ❖ 1 tbsp. of kosher salt
- ❖ Black pepper
- ❖ Oil to coat turkey
- ❖ 1 ½ cups of chicken broth
- ❖ ¾ cup of flour

Cooking Instructions:

1. Remove giblets and neck bones from the turkey cavity and pat the turkey dry.

2. Push the butter slices and garlic in-between the skin and the turkey breasts. Oil up the turkey and season with salt and pepper.

3. Place the lower rack in the air fryer and spray with oil. Place the turkey breast side down in the air fryer and pour in ½ cup of broth over the turkey. Place the extender ring and lid on the air fryer.

4. Air-Fry at 350°F for about 2½ to 3 hours. At the count of every 30 minutes, baste with chicken broth (the first 2 bastes will be with the remaining broth. After that, baste from the broth & juices at the bottom of the Air-fryer).

5. After cooking for 2 hours, take off the air fryer lid and extender ring. Lift the turkey out, flip to breast side up, and then place back into the Air-fryer.

6. Baste the turkey and then place the extender ring and lid back on and continue cooking until the turkey reaches an internal temperature of 165°F at the thickest parts of the thigh, wings and breast, and the juices run clear when you cut between the leg and the thigh for about 30 minutes to 1 hour).

7. Let it rest for about 15 to 20 minutes. While the turkey rests, make the gravy. Remove the lower rack from the air fryer.

8. Leaving the turkey juices and broth in the Air-fryer, skim the chunks from the drippings and broth.

9. Put the flour in a medium bowl and measure in about 1 cup of the drippings and broth into the flour and whisk thoroughly until smooth.

10. Pour the flour mixture into the Air-fryer basket with the remaining drippings and broth. Whisk again until smooth.

11. Place the Air-fryer lid back on and Air-Fry at 400°F for 10 minutes or until it's thickened, whisking a couple of times while cooking.

12. When done serve and enjoy!

Turkey Meatballs

Preparation time: 5 minutes

Cooking time: 20 minutes

Overall time: 25 minutes

Serves: 4 to 6 people

Recipe Ingredients:

- ❖ 1 pound of ground turkey
- ❖ ½ cup of panko bread crumbs
- ❖ 1 egg
- ❖ ¼ cup of fresh parsley
- ❖ 1 tbsp. of low sodium soy sauce
- ❖ Ground black pepper

Cooking Instructions:

1. Mix ingredients in a bowl and stir. Lightly spray air fryer basket and place half of the meatballs in basket.

2. Cook meatballs at 400°F for about 5 minutes then turn the meatballs over and cook for another 5 minutes.

3. Remove cooked meatballs and place the remaining uncooked meatballs in the air fryer basket and repeat.

4. Cook for 5 minutes at 400°F, flip and cook for another 5 minutes.

5. When it's done serve immediately and enjoy!

Turkey Bacon

Preparation time: 5 minutes

Cooking time: 10 minutes

Overall time: 15 minutes

Serves: 2 to 4 people

Recipe Ingredients:

- ❖ 1 package of 8 oz.(Uncured Turkey Bacon)

Cooking Instructions:

1. Preheat Air-fryer at 360ºF. Slice turkey bacon slices in half and place as many pieces that will fit in a single layer in Air-fryer basket.

2. Steam for about 5 minutes, then open Air-fryer and turn the bacon over.

3. Place basket back in Air-fryer and continue to cook for 5 more minutes or until bacon is cooked to your satisfaction.

4. Repeat with remaining bacon pieces until it is all cooked.

5. Serve immediately and enjoy!

Turkey Breakfast Sausage Links

Preparation: 5 minutes

Cooking time: 6 minutes

Overall time: 11 minutes

Serves: 2 to 6 people

Recipe Ingredients:

9.6 oz. package of turkey breakfast sausage links

Cooking Instructions:

1. Preheat your Air-fryer at 350ºF. Then place all 12 links in a single layer in the basket of the Air-fryer.

2. Cook for about 6 minutes. When ready, serve immediately and enjoy!

Amazing Buttermilk Air-Fried Chicken

Preparation time: 15 minutes

Cooking time: 20 minutes

Overall time: 35 minutes

Serves: 6 people

Recipe Ingredients:

- 1 cup of buttermilk
- ½ tsp. of hot sauce
- ⅓ cup of tapioca flour
- ½ tsp. of garlic salt
- ⅛ tsp. of ground black pepper
- 1 egg
- ½ cup of all-purpose flour
- 2 tsp. of salt
- 1 ½ tsp. of brown sugar
- 1 tsp. of garlic powder
- ½ tsp. of paprika
- ½ tsp. of onion powder
- ¼ tsp. of oregano
- ¼ tsp. of black pepper
- 1 lb. of skinless, boneless chicken thighs

Cooking Instructions:

1. Mix buttermilk and hot sauce in a shallow dish and stir thoroughly to combine.

2. Combine tapioca flour, garlic salt, and 1/8 teaspoon of black pepper in a re-sealable plastic bag and shake vigorously to combine.

3. Beat egg in a shallow bowl. After that, mix flour, salt, brown sugar, garlic powder, paprika, onion powder, oregano, and ¼ teaspoon of black pepper in a gallon-sized re-sealable bag and shake to combine.

4. Dip chicken thighs into the prepared ingredients in the following order: buttermilk mixture, tapioca mixture, egg, and flour mixture, shake off excess after each dipping.

5. Preheat your air fryer at 380ºF and line the air fryer basket with parchment paper.

6. Place coated chicken thighs in batches into the air fryer basket and fry for 10 minutes.

7. Turn chicken thighs and fry until chicken is no longer pink in the center and the juices run clear, for additional 10 minutes.

8. Serve and enjoy!

Crumbed Chicken Tenderloins

Preparation time: 15 minutes

Cooking time: 12 minutes

Overall time: 27 minutes

Serves: 2 to 4 people

Recipe Ingredients

- ❖ 1 egg
- ❖ ½ cup of dry bread crumbs
- ❖ 2 tbsp. of vegetable oil
- ❖ 8 eaches of chicken tenderloins

Cooking Instructions:

1. Preheat your air fryer at 350°F and then whisk your egg in a small bowl.

2. Mix-up bread crumbs and oil together in a second bowl until mixture becomes loose and crumbly.

3. Dip each chicken tenderloin into the bowl of egg; shake off any remaining egg.

4. Dip chicken into the crumb mixture, making sure it is evenly and fully covered.

5. Lay chicken tenderloins into the basket of the air-fryer and cook until it's no longer pink in the center for about 12 minutes.

6. An instant-read thermometer inserted into the center should read at least 165°F to check the internal temperature.

7. Serve immediately and enjoy!

Simple Air Fryer Chicken Tenders Recipe

Preparation time: 35 minutes

Cooking time: 12 minutes

Overall time: 47 minutes

Serves: 4 to 6 people

Recipe Ingredients

- 1 pound of chicken tenders
- ½ cup of buttermilk
- ½ cup of panko breadcrumbs
- ½ cup of all-purpose flour
- ¼ teaspoon of baking powder
- ½ teaspoon of salt
- ½ teaspoon of celery seed
- ¼ teaspoon of dried oregano
- 1/8 teaspoon of cayenne
- 1 teaspoon of paprika
- ¼ teaspoon of garlic powder
- ¼ teaspoon of dried thyme
- ½ teaspoon of ground ginger
- ½ teaspoon of ground black pepper
- Olive oil spray

Cooking Instructions:

1. Place the chicken tenders in a zip-lock bag and pour the buttermilk into the bag.

2. Squeeze the air out and seal the bag, let it preserve in the refrigerator for about 30 minutes.

3. In a shallow bowl mix the panko bread crumbs, flour, baking powder, and spices.

4. Remove the chicken strips from the buttermilk with a fork, shake off excess buttermilk, and dredge in the breadcrumb mixture to coat on all sides.

5. Spray the bottom of the air fryer pan. After that put the chicken fingers in the air fryer basket, lightly spray with olive oil spray, then air fry at 375°F for about 10 to 12 minutes until internal temperature reads 175°F and the chicken tenders are golden brown and crispy.

6. Flip the chicken at about half way through cooking time. By making your chicken tenders in batches, simply keep cooked chicken warm in a 170° oven.

7. If need be, you can re-crisp in the Air-fryer for a minute.

8. Serve with your favorite dip and enjoy!

Extra Crispy Gluten-Free Air Fryer Popcorn Chicken

Preparation time: 5 minutes

Cooking time: 10 minutes

Overall time: 10 minutes

Serves: 2 to 3

Recipe Ingredients:

- ❖ 1 pound of skinless chicken tenders (cut into small cubes)
- ❖ ½ cup of corn starch
- ❖ 1 cup of unsweetened lite culinary coconut milk
- ❖ 1 teaspoon of pickle juice
- ❖ 3 cups of finely crushed gluten-free corn flake cereal
- ❖ ½ teaspoon of garlic powder
- ❖ 1/2 teaspoon of onion powder
- ❖ 1/2 teaspoon of paprika
- ❖ ¼ teaspoon of black pepper
- ❖ ¼ teaspoon of cayenne pepper (optional)

Cooking Instructions:

1. Once you've cubed your chicken tenders, place them to the side and set up your 3 coating stations, in order.

2. Firstly, make a plate of the corn starch, secondly, mix-up the coconut milk and pickle juice together in a bowl and stir.

3. Thirdly, crush your corn flakes with the spices in a plastic bag before pouring out onto a plate.

4. Now take each chicken piece, coat in the corn starch, then dunk in the coconut milk, and finally roll in the corn flake crumbs before placing in your Air-fryer basket.

5. Repeat for all the pieces of chicken, evenly spacing them out in the Air-fryer basket (you may need to make two batches depending on the size of your Air-fryer.)

6. Close the Air-fryer and set the temperature at 400°F and the time to 10 minutes (7 to 8 minutes if doing two batches). Once ready serve and enjoy!

BEEF, PORK AND LAMB RECIPES

Gluten Free Air-Fryer Glazed Steaks

Preparation time: 4 hrs.20 minutes

Cooking time: 20 minutes

Overall time: 4 hrs. 40 minutes

Recipe Ingredients:

- ❖ 2 Sirloin steaks at least 6oz.
- ❖ 2 tablespoons of Soy Sauce
- ❖ ½ tablespoon of worcestershire sauce
- ❖ 2 tablespoons of brown sugar
- ❖ 1 table spoon of grated peeled ginger
- ❖ 1 tablespoon garlic crushed
- ❖ 1 teaspoon of seasoned Salt
- ❖ Salt/pepper to taste

Cooking Instructions:

1. In a large seal-able bag, add the steaks along with the remaining ingredients.

2. Seal it up and let it marinate in the fridge for at least 4 hours.

3. Place foil in the bottom of the air fryer, spray with non-stick cooking spray, and then place steaks on it.

4. Cook steaks at 400°F for 10 minutes. Rotate steaks and cook for an additional 10 to 15 minutes or until your desired doneness.

5. When ready serve and enjoy!

Pork Belly Bites

Preparation time: 15 minutes

Cooking time: 15 minutes

Overall time: 30 minutes

Serves: 2 to 4 people

Recipe Ingredients:

- ❖ 1 pound of pork belly, rinsed and patted dry
- ❖ 1 tsp. of Worcestershire sauce or soy sauce
- ❖ ½ tsp. of garlic powder
- ❖ Salt
- ❖ Black pepper, to taste
- ❖ ¼ cup of BBQ sauce (if needed)

Cooking Instructions:

1. Preheat the Air-fryer at 400°F for 4 minutes. After that, remove the skin from the pork belly, if needed.

2. Cut the pork belly into ¾ sized cubes and place in a bowl and season with Worcestershire sauce, garlic powder, salt and pepper.

3. Spread the pork belly in even layer in Air-fryer basket and air-fry at 400°F for about 10 to 18 minutes.

4. Shake and flip pork belly 2 times through cooking process (time depends on your preferred doneness, thickness of the pork belly, size and cooking intensity of your air-fryer).

5. Check the pork belly to see how well done it is cooked, if you want it more done, add an extra 2 to 5 minutes of cooking time.

6. Season with additional salt and pepper if desired. Drizzle with optional BBQ sauce if also desired.

7. Serve warm and enjoy!

Pork Chops

Preparation time: 5 minutes

Cooking time: 15 minutes

Overall time: 20 minutes

Serves: 4 people

Recipe Ingredients:

- ❖ 4 boneless pork chops
- ❖ 2 tablespoons of extra-virgin olive oil
- ❖ ½ freshly grated parmesan
- ❖ 1 teaspoon of kosher salt
- ❖ 1 teaspoon of paprika
- ❖ 1 teaspoon of garlic powder
- ❖ 1 teaspoon of onion powder
- ❖ ½ teaspoon of freshly ground black pepper

Cooking Directions:

- ❖ Pat pork chops dry with paper towels, and then coat both sides with oil.

- ❖ In a medium bowl, combine parmesan and spices. Coat both sides of pork chops with Parmesan mixture.

- ❖ Place pork chops in basket of air fryer and cook at 375°F for 9 minutes, flipping halfway through.

- ❖ Serve immediately and enjoy!

Pork Steak

Preparation time: 1 minute

Cooking time: 8 minutes

Overall time: 9 minutes

Serves: 2 people

Recipe Ingredients:

- ❖ 2 pork steaks
- ❖ Salt and pepper

Cooking Instructions:

1. Place your Air-fryer pork steaks into your Air-fryer grill or Air-fryer basket, making sure that they are not overlapping.

2. Season with salt and pepper from within the air fryer basket. Close the air fryer and cook for about 8 minutes at 360°F.

3. Serve with your favourite pork steak sides.

Pork Schnitzel

Preparation time: 10 minutes

Cooking time: 14 minutes

Overall time: 24 minutes

Recipe Ingredients:

- ❖ 4 boneless pork chops, (cut into 1/3 thickness)
- ❖ ¼ tsp. of thyme
- ❖ 1/8 tsp. of garlic salt
- ❖ ¼ tsp. of old bay seasoning
- ❖ ¼ tsp. of dried sage
- ❖ ¼ tsp. of minced rosemary
- ❖ 1 large egg
- ❖ ½ cup of flour
- ❖ Salt and pepper to taste
- ❖ 2/3 cup of panko

Cooking Instructions:

1. Rinse and pat dry the pork chops, then turn on your air-fryer at 390°F while creating a dipping station.

2. In one bowl mix panko and spices thoroughly to combine well, add a small amount of salt and pepper to taste. Place egg and flour in two separate bowls.

3. Dip chop in flour to coat, then into egg wash. Now dredge all sides of the pork into the panko mixture. Finish all pork chops and coat all surfaces.

4. Spray the basket from the air fryer with olive oil spray then place into the air fryer basket.

5. Place them into the basket and cook for 12 to 14 minutes opening at 8 minutes, spraying with a light burst of oil to help get a golden brown color.

6. Check temperature to make sure it is 145° or cut into them and check to make sure the pork is opaque. Cook in batches if you have more. Serve immediately.

Pork Cutlets

Preparation time: 15 minutes

Cooking time: 9 minutes

Overall time: 18 minutes

Serves: 3 to 4 people

Recipe Ingredients:

- ❖ 4 boneless pork sirloin chops, cut into ¼-inch thickness
- ❖ 1 teaspoon of salt
- ❖ ½ teaspoon of pepper
- ❖ 1 cup of flour
- ❖ 2 eggs
- ❖ 1 cup of non-seasoned bread crumbs
- ❖ 2 tablespoons of olive oil

Cooking Instructions:

1. Place one pork chop between two pieces of plastic wrap and pound to ¼-inch thickness. Repeat with remaining chops.

2. Season both sides of each of the pork cutlets with salt and pepper. On your work surface, line up three shallow bowls (cake or pie pans are perfect).

3. In the first bowl, place the flour, in the second, whisk together the eggs and in the third, combine the breadcrumbs and olive oil. Mix-up thoroughly to coat all bread crumbs with the oil.

4. Start by dredging both sides of a pork cutlet in the flour, then dipping both sides into the eggs and then coat with the breadcrumb mixture. Repeat with the remaining cutlets.

5. Cook in batches if necessary. Place the breaded pork cutlets in the air fryer basket without overlapping.

6. Set the temperature at 360°F and cook for about 9 minutes. Turn cutlets over half-way through the cooking time.

7. Remove from air fryer basket and keep warm in a pre-heated oven at 185°F.Repeat until all pork cutlets are cooked.

8. Serve and enjoy with buttered noodles, red cabbage sauerkraut, or French fries.

Pork Roast

Preparation time: 10 minutes

Cooking time: 1 hr 20 minutes

Overall time: 1 hr 30 minutes

Serves: 2 to 4

Recipe Ingredients:

- ❖ 1.2kg of pork shoulder
- ❖ 1 kg sweet potatoes
- ❖ 1 tablespoon of olive oil
- ❖ 1 tablespoon of thyme
- ❖ Salt and pepper

Cooking Instructions:

1. Score your pork roast with similar sized square slits, season pork with salt and pepper and load it onto the rotisserie.

2. Place in your air fryer oven and cook for 1 hour at 360°F. While your pork roast is cooking, peel your sweet potatoes and chop into roasted sweet potato shapes.

3. Season with thyme, salt and pepper. Add in extra virgin olive oil and in a bowl mix thoroughly with your hands so that the olive oil is well coated on the sweet potatoes.

4. Cook for about 15 minutes at 320°F, shake and then cook for a further 5 minutes at 400°F.

5. Slice your pork once it beeps and serve with your air fryer roasted sweet potatoes.

Mongolian Beef

Preparation time: 20 minutes

Cooking time: 20 minutes

Overall time: 40 minutes

Serves: 4 to 6 people

Recipe Ingredients:

- ❖ Meat
- ❖ 1 pound of flank steak
- ❖ ¼ cup of corn starch
- ❖ Sauce
- ❖ 2 teaspoons of vegetable oil
- ❖ ½ teaspoon of ginger
- ❖ 1 table of minced garlic
- ❖ ½ cup of soy sauce or gluten free soy sauce
- ❖ ½ cup of water
- ❖ ¾ cup brown sugar, packed
- ❖ Cooked rice
- ❖ Green beans
- ❖ Green onions

Cooking Instructions:

1. Thinly slice the steak in long pieces and then coat it with the corn starch.

2. Place in the Air-fryer and cook at 390ºF for 5 minutes on each side. (Add extra 5 minutes if needed).

3. While the steak cooks, warm up all sauce ingredients in a medium sized saucepan on medium-high heat.

4. Whisk the ingredients together until it gets to a low boil. Once both the steak and sauce are cooked, place the steak in a bowl with the sauce and let it soak in for about 5 to 10 minutes.

5. When ready to serve, use tongs to remove the steak and let the excess sauce drip off.

6. Now place steak on cooked rice and green beans, top with additional sauce if you desire. Enjoy!

Korean BBQ Beef

Preparation time: 15 minutes

Cooking time: 30 minutes

Overall time: 45 minutes

Serves: 5 to 6 people

Recipe Ingredients:

- ❖ Meat
- ❖ 1 pound of flank steak or thinly sliced steak
- ❖ ¼ cup of corn starch
- ❖ Pompeian oils coconut spray
- ❖ Sauce
- ❖ ½cup of soy sauce or gluten-free soy sauce
- ❖ ½cup brown sugar
- ❖ 2 tablespoons of pompeian white wine vinegar
- ❖ 1 clove of garlic, crushed
- ❖ 1 table of spoon hot chili sauce
- ❖ 1 tablespoon of ground ginger
- ❖ ½ teaspoon of sesame seeds
- ❖ 1 tablespoon of cornstarch
- ❖ 1 tablespoon of water

Cooking Instructions:

1. Begin by preparing the steak. Then thinly slice it then toss in the cornstarch.

2. Spray the basket or line it with foil in the Air-fryer with coconut oil spray. After that, add the steak and spray another coat of spray on top.

3. Cook in the Air-fryer for about 10 minutes at 390ºF, turn the steak and cook for an additional 10 minutes.

4. While the steak is cooking add the sauce ingredients except the cornstarch and water to a medium saucepan.

5. Warm it up to a low boil, then whisk in the cornstarch and water. Carefully remove steak and pour sauce over the steak, stir thoroughly to combine.

6. Serve and enjoy topped with sliced green onions, cooked rice, and green beans.

Rib Eye Steak with Blue Cheese

Preparation time: 15 minutes

Cooking time: 7 minutes

Resting time: 5 minutes

Overall time: 22 minutes

Recipe Ingredients:

- ❖ 32 oz.rib eye steaks (two steaks-1 inch thick)
- ❖ 2 tsp. of kosher salt
- ❖ Tsp. of freshly ground black pepper
- ❖ 1 tsp. of garlic powder
- ❖ 2 tbsp. of blue cheese butter

Cooking Instructions:

1. Prepare Blue Cheese Butter according to directions. Remove rib eye steaks from refrigerator for 15 minutes before starting recipe.

2. Turn Air-fryer to 400ºF (or the highest temperature possible) and set time to 15 minutes.

3. Preheat air fryer at least 5 minutes before placing in steaks. Coat both sides of steaks with salt, garlic powder and pepper.

4. With your hand, press seasonings into steaks, then open your Air-fryer and quickly place both steaks into basket and close it.

5. Cook at 400ºF for about 4 minutes and then quickly flip steaks over and cook for 3 minutes more.

6. Turn off Air-fryer and do not open. Let it sit for 1 minute for rare, for medium rare, let sit 2 minutes, for less rare let it sit for 3 minutes, and so on.

7. Top with blue cheese butter and serve.

Beef Kabobs

Preparation time: 30 minutes

Cooking time: 10 minutes

Overall time: 40 minutes

Serves: 2 to 4 people

Recipe Ingredients:

- ❖ 1 pound of beef chuck ribs cut in 1-inch pieces.
- ❖ 1/3 cup of low-fat sour cream
- ❖ 2 tablespoons soy sauce
- ❖ 1 bell peppers
- ❖ ½ onion
- ❖ 8-to-6-inch skewers

Cooking Instructions:

1. Mix sour cream with soy sauce in a medium bowl. Place beef chunks into the bowl and marinate for at least 30 minutes, better overnight.

2. Cut bell pepper and onion in 1-inch pieces. Soak wooden skewers in water for about 10 minutes.

3. Thread beef, onions and bell peppers onto skewers and add some freshly ground black pepper.

4. Cook in preheated Air-fryer at 400ºF for 10 minutes, turning half way.

5. Serve immediately and enjoy!

Beef Empanadas

Preparation time: 10 minutes

Cooking time: 16 minutes

Overall time: 30 minutes

Serves: 8 people

Recipe Ingredients:

- ❖ 8 Goya empanada discs, in frozen section, thawed
- ❖ 1 cup of picadillo
- ❖ 1 egg white, whisked
- ❖ 1 tsp. water

Cooking Instructions:

1. Preheat your Air-fryer at 325°F for about 8 minutes. Then spray the basket generously with cooking spray.

2. Place 2 tablespoons of picadillo in the center of each disc. Fold in half and use a fork to seal the edges. Repeat with the remaining dough.

3. Whisk the egg whites with water, and then brush the tops of the empanadas.

4. Bake 2 or 3 at a time in the air fryer for 8 minutes, or until it turns golden.

5. Remove from heat and repeat with the remaining empanadas.

6. Serve and enjoy!

Philly Cheese Steak Taquitos

Preparation time: 20 minutes

Cooking time: 8 hours

Overall time: 8 hours 20 minutes

Serves: 4 to 6 people

Recipe Ingredients:

- ❖ 1 pack mission or super soft corn tortillas
- ❖ 3 pounds of beef steak strips
- ❖ 2 green peppers sliced
- ❖ 1 white onion finely chopped
- ❖ 1 package of dry Italian dressing mix
- ❖ 2 cups of beef stock
- ❖ 10 slices of provolone cheese
- ❖ Cooking spray or olive oil

Cooking Instructions:

1. Add beef, onion, bell pepper, seasonings and stock to the slow cooker. Cover and cook on low for about 6 to 8 hours.

2. Heat tortillas in a tortilla warmer for 1 to 2 minutes in the microwave. Once cooked, spoon 2 to 3 tablespoons of cooked cheesesteak in the center of the tortilla- lengthwise across the tortilla.

3. Add a little cheese (amount is a personal preference, but you can use about ¼ of a slice per taquito).

4. Roll tortilla tightly and place in air fryer basket. Repeat with all tortillas.

5. Brush lightly with oil or spray with cooking spray. Cook in a preheated air fryer at 350°F for about 6 to 8 minutes, or until lightly browned

6. Flip halfway through and add more oil.

Lamb Chops

Preparation time: 3 minutes

Cooking time: 25minutes

Overall time: 28 minutes

Serves: 1 or 2people

Recipe Ingredients:

- ❖ 1 to 2 medium lamb chops
- ❖ 100ml lemon juice (optional)

Cooking Instructions:

1. Preheat the Air-fryer to 175°C which frequently takes about 3 minutes depending on the Air-fryer.

2. Place the Lamb Chops in the Air-fryer basket and cook for about 25 minutes.

3. Once cooked, rest the meat for 10 minutes. Serve immediately and enjoy.

Lamb Chops with Horseradish Sauce

Preparation time: 10 minutes

Cooking time: 13 minutes

Preserving time: 30 minutes

Overall time: 53 minutes

Serves: 1 to 2 people

Recipe Ingredients:

- ❖ Lamb chops
- ❖ 4 lamb loin chops
- ❖ 2 tablespoons of vegetable oil
- ❖ 1 clove of minced garlic
- ❖ ½ teaspoon of kosher salt
- ❖ ½ of black pepper
- ❖ Vegetable oil spray for cooking
- ❖ Horseradish cream sauce
- ❖ ½ cup of mayonnaise
- ❖ 1 tablespoon of dijon mustard
- ❖ 1 ½ tablespoons of prepared horseradish
- ❖ 2 teaspoons of sugar

Cooking Instructions:

1. For the lamb: Brush the lamb chops with the oil, rub with the garlic, and sprinkle with the salt and pepper. Preserve at room temperature for 30 minutes.

2. While for the sauce: In a medium bowl, combine the mayonnaise, mustard, horse radish, and sugar and stir until well combined. Set aside half of the sauce for serving.

3. Spray the air fryer basket with vegetable oil spray and place the chops in the basket.

4. Set your Air-fryer to 325°F for 10 minutes, turning the chops halfway through the cooking time.

5. Remove the chops from the air-fryer and add to the bowl with the horse radish sauce, turning it to coat with the sauce.

6. Place the chops back in the air fryer basket and set the air-fryer to 400°F for 3 minutes.

7. Use a meat thermometer to ensure the meat has reached an internal temperature of 145°F (i.e. for medium- rare).

8. Serve the chops with the reserved horseradish sauce and enjoy!

Air Fried Lamb/Spicy Lamb Sirloin Steak/ Tandoori Raan

Preparation time: 40 minutes

Cooking time: 15 minutes

Overall time: 55 minutes

Serves: 2 to 4 people

Recipe Ingredients:

- ½ onion
- 4 slices of ginger
- 5 cloves of garlic
- 1 tsp. of garam masala
- 1 tsp. of ground fennel
- 1 tsp. of ground cinnamon
- ½ tsp. of ground cardamom
- ½ 1 tsp. of cayenne pepper
- 1 tsp. of kosher salt
- 1 lb. of boneless lamb sirloin steaks

Cooking Instructions:

1. Into a blender bowl, add all ingredients except the lamb chops. Pulse and blend for 4 minutes or until the onion is minced fine and all ingredients are blended.

2. Place the lamb chops into a large bowl. Use a knife to slash into the meat and fat to allow the marinade to penetrate better.

3. Add the blended spice paste and mix thoroughly. Allow the mixture to rest for about 30 minutes or up to 24 hours in a refrigerator.

4. Preheat your Air-fryer at 330°F for about 15 minutes and place the lamb steaks in a single layer in the Air-fryer basket and cook, flipping half way through.

5. Use a meat thermometer; ensure that the meat has reached an internal temperature of 150°F for medium well.

6. Serve immediately.

Lamb meatballs

Preparation time: 10 minutes

Cooking time: 22 minutes

Overall time: 33 minutes

Serves: 5 to 10 people

Recipe Ingredients:

- ❖ 1 pound of ground buy ranch direct lamb
- ❖ couple sprays of avocado oil spray
- ❖ ½ tablespoon of fourth and heart california garlic ghee
- ❖ 1 red bell of diced pepper
- ❖ 1/3 cup of diced red onion
- ❖ 1/3 cup of diced cilantro
- ❖ 1/3 cup of diced zucchini
- ❖ 1 tablespoon of primal palate super gyro seasoning
- ❖ ½ teaspoon of turmeric
- ❖ ½ teaspoon of cumin
- ❖ ½ teaspoon coriander
- ❖ 2 garlic cloves minced
- ❖ Salt and pepper to taste

Cooking Instructions:

1. Add your veggies to a food processor and pulse for a couple times to dice.

2. Sauté your veggies for 5 to 7 minutes with ghee and let it cool completely

3. Season your lamb with super gyro seasoning, turmeric, coriander, cumin, salt, pepper and garlic.

4. Add sautéed veggies to lamb, mix with hands, and form into meatballs then spray your air fryer rack with avocado oil spray.

5. Add meatballs and cook in air fryer at 370°F for 15 minutes. You can also cook in a pan or bake 350° for 20 minutes.

6. When ready, serve and enjoy!

Greek lamb burger with chips

Preparation time: 10 minutes

Cooking time: 20 minutes

Overall time: 30 minutes

Serves: 2 to 4

Recipe Ingredients:

- 1.5 pounds of ground lamb
- 1 tsp. of oregano
- 1/3 cup of feta cheese, crumbled
- ½ tsp. salt and pepper
- 4 buns
- ½ head lettuce
- 1 medium tomato
- 1 cup of tzatziki sauce

Cooking Instructions:

1. Make tzatziki sauce and keep ready when you start your burgers. Turn your Air-fryer on at 375°F and preheat for 5 minutes.

2. In a medium bowl thoroughly mix together ground lamb, oregano, crumbled feta cheese and pepper.

3. Once completely blended form it into four 6 ounce patties making sure they are of the same thickness.

4. Once the burgers are formed, sprinkle outsides with salt and pepper. After that, spray the basket with olive oil to prevent sticking.

5. Place all burgers in a single layer on the basket of the air fryer. If your air fryer is small you may cook in batches.

6. Cook for about 8 to 10 minutes per side, flipping at 10 minutes interval. Use a thermometer to cook to an internal temperature at 160°F.

7. Remove from Air-fryer and allow it to rest for 5 minutes to permit juices to settle.

8. Serve each burger atop a brioche bun, alongside a tray of lettuce leaves and tomato slices.

9. Serve each burger topped with 2 tablespoons of the tzatziki sauce.

Roasted Leg of Lamb with Garlic and Rosemary

Preparation time: 5 minutes

Cooking time: 30 minutes

Overall time: 35 minutes

Serves: 6 to 7 people

Recipe Ingredients:

- ❖ 3 lb. leg of lamb
- ❖ 3 tbsp. of minced garlic
- ❖ 1 tbsp. salt
- ❖ 2 tbsp. of minced fresh rosemary
- ❖ ½ tsp. of black pepper
- ❖ ¼ cup of beef broth
- ❖ 2 tbsp. of olive oil

Cooking Instructions:

1. In a small bowl, mix-up the minced garlic, salt, rosemary, black pepper, beef broth, and olive oil thoroughly to combine.

2. Rub the seasoning mix all over the lamb. Then set the lamb into the Air-fryer for 25 minutes at 350°F.

3. Check with a meat thermometer and make sure that the temperature is 130°F before you remove it.

4. Serve immediately!

Baby Back Ribs

Preparation time: 15 minutes

Cooking time: 35 minutes

Extra time: 30 minutes

Overall time: 1 hour 20 minutes

Serves: 2 to 4 people

Recipe Ingredients:

- 1 rack of baby back ribs
- 1 tbsp. of olive oil
- 1 tbsp. of liquid smoke flavoring
- 1 tbsp. of brown sugar
- ½ tsp. of salt
- ½ tsp. of ground black pepper
- ½ tsp. of garlic powder
- ½ tsp. of onion powder
- ½ tsp. of chili powder
- 1 cup of BBQ sauce

Cooking Instructions:

1. Remove membrane from back of ribs and dry ribs with a paper towel. Cut rack into 4 pieces.

2. Mix olive oil and liquid smoke in a small bowl and rub on both sides of the ribs.

3. Combine brown sugar, salt, pepper, garlic powder, onion powder and chili powder in a bowl.

4. Season both sides of the ribs generously with seasoning mix and let ribs rest for 30 minutes to enhance the flavor. Then preheat Air-fryer to 375ºF.

5. Place ribs bone-side down in your Air-fryer basket, making sure they are not touching; cook in batches if necessary.

6. Cook for 15 minutes, flip ribs over and cook for extra 10 minutes. Remove ribs from air fryer and brush bone-side of ribs with ½ cup of BBQ sauce.

7. Place basket back in the Air-fryer and cook for more 5 minutes. Flip ribs over, brush meat-side with remaining ½ cup of BBQ sauce then cook for 5 minutes or until desired doneness is achieved.

8. Now serve and enjoy!

SNACK AND SIDE DISHES RECIPES

Green Bean and Mushroom 'Casserole'

Preparation time: 10 minutes

Cooking time: 10 minutes

Overall time: 20 minutes

Serves: 4 to 6 people

Recipe Ingredients:

- ❖ 24 oz. of fresh green beans - trimmed
- ❖ 2 cups of sliced button mushrooms
- ❖ 1 fresh lemon juiced
- ❖ 1 tbsp. of garlic powder
- ❖ 3/4 tsp. of ground sage
- ❖ 1 tsp. of onion powder
- ❖ 3/4 tsp. of salt
- ❖ 3/4 tsp. of black pepper
- ❖ Spray oil
- ❖ 1/3 cup of french fried onions (optional)

Cooking Instructions:

- ❖ In a large bowl, toss together the green beans, mushrooms, lemon juice, garlic powder, sage, onion powder, salt, and pepper.

- ❖ Transfer the mixture to your Air-fryer basket, then use spray oil to coat, shaking well.

- ❖ Air-fry at 400°F for about 10 to 12 minutes, shaking every 2 to 3 minutes.

- ❖ Serve topped with French fried onions, if you're using them.

Honey and Balsamic Air Fryer Brussels Sprouts

Preparation time: 8 minutes

Cooking time: 10 minutes

Overall time: 18 minutes

Recipe Ingredients:

- ❖ 1 lb. of brussels sprouts, cleaned and halved
- ❖ 2 tbsp. of olive oil
- ❖ Salt and pepper, to taste
- ❖ 2 tbsp. of honey
- ❖ 2 tbsp. of balsamic vinegar

Cooking Instructions:

1. Mix-up brussels sprouts in bowl with olive oil, salt and pepper thoroughly.

2. Transfer brussels sprouts to Air-fryer basket and cook at 400°F for 8 to 10 minutes, shaking the basket halfway through cooking time.

3. Toss brussels sprouts with honey and balsamic vinegar immediately before serving.

4. Serve warm and enjoy!

Acorn Squash

Preparation time: 5 minutes

Cooking time: 15 minutes

Overall time: 20 minutes

Serves: 4 to 6 people

Recipe Ingredients:

- ❖ 1 Acorn squash
- ❖ 1 tbsp. of avocado oil
- ❖ 1 teaspoon poultry seasoning
- ❖ Salt and pepper to taste

Cooking Instructions:

1. Cut one acorn squash down the middle length wise. Scrape out the seeds with a spoon and discard them.

2. Slice the acorn squash into 1 thick slice. As you get down to the smaller pieces, they may not be the same size.

3. In a bowl, toss together acorn squash slices, avocado oil, poultry seasoning, salt and pepper.

4. Grease the bottom of your air fryer basket and add acorn slices in. Do not overcrowd your air fryer basket.

5. Air-fry at 375°F for 15 minutes and serve hot.

Chanukkah Latkes

Preparation time: 18 minutes

Cooking time: 9 minutes

Overall time: 27 minutes

Recipe Ingredients:

- ❖ 5 large potatoes peeled or unpeeled
- ❖ 1 large yellow/brown onion
- ❖ 4 large eggs
- ❖ 1/3 cup of matzo meal
- ❖ ¼ cup of potato starch (divided)- "if desired"
- ❖ 2 tsp. kosher salt
- ❖ ½ tsp. of freshly ground black pepper
- ❖ ½ tsp. baking powder (optional)
- ❖ Grape-seed oil vegetable oil or extra virgin olive oil

Cooking Instructions:

1. Scrub Potatoes well and peel if you like. Then run potatoes through food processor to grate and then place in a Bowl with cool waters and set aside.

2. Rinse out food processor and shred or grate onions. After that, place onion in tea towel or cheesecloth and squeeze out all liquid.

3. In a medium mixing bowl, whisk together eggs thoroughly and add salt, pepper, matzo meal, 1 tablespoon of potato starch, baking powder (if using) and drained onions.

4. Drain water from potatoes and save the Starch left in the bowl. Squeeze out all water from Potatoes and add to onion mixture.

5. Scoop out the starch from the potato bowl and add to Latkes mixture. Use a cookie scoop and dip into potato starch, if desired.

6. With a spatula, flatten latkes to about ¼ thick, spray one side of Latkes well with oil. Place oil side down in well oiled Air-fryer and generously spray Latkes with oil.

7. Air-Fry at 380ºF for about 9 minutes, turning over after 5 minutes. Serve with applesauce and sour cream.

Zucchini Chips

Preparation time: 10 minutes

Cooking time: 12 minutes

Overall time: 22 minutes

Serves: 2 to 4 people

Recipe Ingredients

- ❖ 1 cup of panko bread crumbs
- ❖ ¾ cup of grated parmesan cheese
- ❖ 1 medium of thinly sliced zucchini
- ❖ 1 large egg, beaten
- ❖ 1 serving cooking spray

Cooking Instructions:

1. Preheat your Air-fryer at 350°F before you begin preparing the zucchini.

2. Combine panko and Parmesan cheese on a plate. Dip 1 zucchini slice into beaten egg then into panko mixture, pressing it to coat.

3. Place zucchini slice on a wire baking rack and repeat with remaining slices. Lightly spray zucchini slices with cooking spray.

4. Place as many zucchini slices in the air fryer basket as you can without overlapping them.

5. Cook for 10 minutes while flipping with tongs and cook for 2 minute more. After that, remove from air fryer and repeat with remaining zucchini slices.

6. When done serve warm and enjoy!

Air-Fried Taco Dogs

Preparation time: 5 minutes

Cooking time: 10 minutes

Overall time: 15 minutes

Serves: 2 people

Recipe Ingredients:

- ❖ 2 eaches jumbo of hot dogs
- ❖ 1 tsp. of taco seasoning mix
- ❖ 2 roll (blank)s of hot dog buns
- ❖ ⅓ cup of guacamole
- ❖ 4 tbsp. of salsa
- ❖ 6 slice (blank)s of pickled jalapeno slices

Cooking Instructions:

1. Preheat an Air-fryer to 390°F and make sure the air-fryer is at temperature for at least 4 minutes.

2. Cut 5 slits into each hot dog and evenly rub ½ teaspoon taco seasoning over each hot dog.

3. Cook hot dogs in the air-fryer basket for 5 minutes. After that, place hot dogs in buns and return to the basket.

4. Cook until buns are toasted and hot dogs are crisp, for about 4 minutes more.

5. Top hot dogs with equal amounts of guacamole, salsa, and jalapenos.

6. Serve and enjoy!

Potato Hay

Preparation time: 10 minutes

Cooking time: 30 minutes

Extra time: 20 minutes

Overall time: 1 hour

Serves: 4 to 6 people

Recipe Ingredients:

- ❖ 2 eaches russet potatoes
- ❖ 1 tbsp. of canola oil
- ❖ 1 pinch of kosher salt and ground black pepper to taste

Cooking Instructions:

1. Cut potatoes into spirals using the medium grating attachment on a spiralizer, cutting the spirals with kitchen shears after 4 or 5 rotations.

2. Soak potato spirals in a bowl of water for 20 minutes. After that, drain and rinse well.

3. Pat potatoes dry with paper towels, removing as much moisture as possible.

4. Place potatoes spirals in a large re-sealable plastic bag and add oil, salt, and pepper; then toss to coat.

5. Preheat your Air-fryer at 360ºF, then place half of the potato spirals in the fry basket and insert into the air fryer. Cook until golden, for about 5 minutes.

6. Increase temperature to 390ºF. Pull out the fry basket and toss potato spirals using tongs.

7. Return basket to the Air-fryer and continue cooking, tossing occasionally, until golden brown for about 10 to 12 minutes.

8. Reduce temperature to 360ºF and repeat with remaining potato spirals. Yummy!

Avocado Fries

Preparation time: 10 minutes

Cooking time: 10 minutes

Overall time: 20 minutes

Serves: 2 people

Recipe Ingredients:

- ¼ cup all-purpose flour
- ½ tsp. of ground black pepper
- ¼ tsp. of salt
- 1 egg
- 1 tsp. of water
- 1 ripe avocado, halved, seeded, peeled and cut into 8 slices
- ½ cup of panko bread crumbs
- 1 serving cooking spray

Cooking Instructions:

1. Preheat Air-fryer at 400°F and mix flour, pepper, and salt together in a shallow bowl.

2. Beat together egg and water in a second shallow bowl and place panko in a third shallow bowl.

3. Dredge an avocado slice through the flour, shaking off excess flour, dip into egg and allow excess to drop off.

4. Finally press slice into panko so both sides are covered. Set on a plate and repeat with the remaining slices.

5. Spray avocado slices generously with cooking spray and arrange in the bowl of the air fryer, sprayed-side down.

6. Spray the top side of the avocado slices as well then cook in the preheated air fryer for about 4 minutes.

7. Turn avocado slices over and cook until it turns golden for about 3 more minutes.

8. Serve, plate and enjoy!

Sweet Potato Chips

Preparation time: 10 minutes

Cooking time: 13 minutes

Overall time: 23 minutes

Serves: 1 to people

Recipe Ingredients:

- ❖ 1 tsp. of avocado oil
- ❖ 1 medium sweet potato, peeled and sliced crossways into 1/8-inch slices
- ❖ ½ tsp. of creole seasoning, or to taste

Cooking Instructions:

1. Preheat your Air-fryer at 400°F and place sweet potato slices in a large bowl.

2. Stir in avocado oil evenly coating each piece. Then add Creole seasoning, stirring to combine well.

3. Place slices in a thin layer on the bottom of the air fryer basket and cook in the preheated air fryer for about 7 minutes.

4. Shake slices and turn to allow for even cooking. Continue cooking until desired crispness is achieved for about 6 more minutes.

5. Transfer potato slices to a rack and allow it to cool.

6. Serve immediately.

Sweet Potato Tots

Preparation time: 15 minutes

Cooking time: 35 minutes

Extra time: 10 minutes

Overall time: 1 hour

Serves: 4 to 8 people

Recipe Ingredients:

- ❖ 2 eaches of sweet potatoes, peeled
- ❖ ½ tsp. of cajun seasoning
- ❖ 1 serving olive oil cooking spray
- ❖ 1 pinch of sea salt to taste

Cooking Instructions:

1. Bring a pot of water to a boil and add sweet potatoes. Boil until potatoes can be pierced with a fork but are still firm, for about 15 minutes.

2. Do not over-boil, or they will be messy to grate then drain and let it cool.

3. Grate sweet potatoes into a bowl using a box grater. Carefully mix in Cajun seasoning. After that form mixture into tot-shaped cylinders.

4. Spray the Air-fryer basket with olive oil spray and place tots in the basket in a single row without touching each other or the sides of the basket.

5. Spray tots with olive oil spray and sprinkle with sea salt. Heat Air-fryer at 400°F and cook tots for 8 minutes.

6. Turn, spray with more olive oil spray, and sprinkle with more sea salt and cook for 8 minutes more.

7. When ready serve and enjoy!

Spicy Dill Pickle Fries

Preparation time: 15 minutes

Cooking time: 15 minutes

Overall time: 30 minutes

Serves: 10 to 12 people

Recipe Ingredients:

- 1 ½ (16 ounce) jars of spicy dill pickle spears
- 1 cup of all-purpose flour
- ½ teaspoon of paprika
- ¼ cup of milk
- 1 egg, beaten
- 1 cup of panko bread crumbs
- 1 serving cooking spray

Cooking Instructions:

1. Drain pickles and pat dry. Combine flour and paprika in a bowl, Combine milk and beaten egg in another bowl and place panko in a third bowl.

2. Heat your Air-fryer at 400ºF according to manufacturer's instructions.

3. Dip a pickle first in flour mixture, then in egg mixture, and then in bread crumbs until thoroughly coated and place on a plate.

4. Repeat with remaining pickles. Spray coated pickles lightly with cooking spray.

5. Place pickles in a single layer in the Air-fryer basket and cook in batches if necessary to avoid overcrowding the fryer.

6. Set time to 14 minutes and turn pickles halfway through cooking time.

7. Serve immediately.

Air-Fried Mozzarella Sticks

Preparation time: 20 minutes

Cooking: 15 minutes

Extra time: 1 hour

Overall time: 1 hour 35 minutes

Serves: 2 to 4 people

Recipe Ingredients:

Batter:

- ½ cup of water
- ¼ cup of all-purpose flour
- 5 tbsp. of cornstarch
- 1 tbsp. of cornmeal
- 1 tsp. of garlic powder
- ½ tsp. of salt

Coating:

- 1 cup of panko bread crumbs
- ½ tsp. of salt
- ½ tsp. of ground black pepper
- ½ tsp. of parsley flakes
- ½ tsp. of garlic powder
- ¼ tsp. of onion powder
- ¼ tsp. of dried oregano
- ¼ tsp. of dried basil
- 5 oz. of mozzarella cheese, cut into ½-inch strips
- 1 tbsp. of all-purpose flour, or as needed
- 1 serving cooking spray

Cooking Instructions:

1. Place water, flour, cornstarch, cornmeal, garlic powder, and salt in a wide, shallow bowl; mix into a batter the consistency of pancake batter.

2. Adjust ingredients if needed to get the right consistency.Stir panko, salt, pepper, parsley, garlic powder, onion powder, oregano, and basil together in another wide, shallow bowl.

3. Lightly coat each mozzarella stick with flour. Dip each stick in the batter and toss in the panko mixture until fully coated.

4. Place sticks in a single layer on a baking sheet and freeze for at least 1 hour.

5. Heat your Air-fryer to 400°F according to manufacturer's instructions. Then place a row of mozzarella sticks in the fryer basket and spray with a light coat of cooking spray.

6. Cook sticks for 6 minutes. After 6 minutes, open fryer and flip the sticks with tongs. Continue cooking for about 7 to 9 minutes until it turns golden brown.

7. Serve immediately!

Fried Pickles

Preparation time: 5 minutes

Cooking time: 25 minutes

Overall time: 30 minutes

Serves: 2 to 4 people

Recipe Ingredients:

- ❖ 1 jar of whole kosher dill pickles
- ❖ ½ cup of milk
- ❖ An egg
- ❖ 1 container of seasoned bread crumbs
- ❖ 1 tablespoon of oil

Cooking Instructions:

1. Remove the pickles from the jar and dry them off using a paper towel. Slice them into ¼ inch to ½ inch slices.

2. Next, make egg wash using ½ cup of milk and 1 egg, whisk thoroughly together.

3. Place ¼ to ½ of the container of bread crumbs into a small bowl and dip the pickle slices into the egg wash, coating both sides.

4. Next, place the pickle slice into the bread crumbs. Once coated on one side, flip to coat the other side.

5. Use the oil to coat the air fryer basket to prevent sticking.

6. Place all the breaded pickles into the basket and set the basket inside the cooker. Set the temperature to 392°F and the timer to 15 minutes.

7. Make sure to flip the pickles halfway through the cooking time. Once the timer rings, carefully remove the basket and allow the fried pickles to cool for 5 minutes.

8. Then serve and enjoy!

Asparagus Fries

Preparation time 5 minutes

Cooking time: 8 minutes

Overall time: 13 minutes

Serves: 2 people

Recipe Ingredients:

- ❖ 16 to 20 spears asparagus
- ❖ 1 medium egg
- ❖ 1 teaspoon of water
- ❖ 1/3 cup of regular breadcrumbs
- ❖ 1/4 cup of panko breadcrumbs
- ❖ 1 tablespoon of garlic powder, onion powder, salt, pepper, poppy seeds(1/8 tsp. each)
- ❖ Oil spray

Cooking Instructions:

1. Prepare the asparagus by cutting or snapping off the hard ends; about 1 inch up the stem and discard those pieces. Wash and dry the asparagus.

2. In a shallow dish, add an egg and a bit of water, then whisk and beat until a little frothy then add the asparagus and toss around to coat.

3. In a separate shallow dish or bowl, add panko breadcrumbs, regular breadcrumbs, and spices.

4. Add the asparagus spears a few at a time, and toss around until coated. Place them into the air fryer tray and repeat until all asparagus are coated.

5. Now add fries to the air fryer basket, do not place them too close together. Lightly spray the tops with oil, and close it.

6. Set air fryer for 400°F for 8 minutes. After 5 minutes, open and carefully flip fries over, then close and cook for the remaining 3 minutes.

7. Serve with your favorite dipping sauce and enjoy!

Easy Garlic Knots

Preparation time: 10 minutes

Cooking time: 20 minutes

Overall time: 30 minutes

Serves: 4 to 8 people

Recipe Ingredients:

- ❖ Olive oil spray
- ❖ 1 cup of all purpose or white whole wheat flour
- ❖ ¾ tsp. of kosher salt (less for table salt)
- ❖ 2 tsp. of baking powder
- ❖ 1 cup of fat free Greek Yogurt, drained of any excess liquid
- ❖ 2 tsp. of butter
- ❖ 3 cloves of garlic, chopped
- ❖ 1 tbsp. of grated parmesan cheese
- ❖ 1 tbsp. of finely chopped fresh parsley

Cooking Instructions:

1. Preheat oven to 375°F. Then line a rimmed baking sheet with a silicone liner or Silpat.

2. In a large bowl combine the flour, baking powder and salt and whisk thoroughly to combine well.

3. Add the yogurt and mix with a spoon until integrated. Then use your dry hands and knead for about 15 times.

4. If it's too sticky you can add a little more flour and roll into a ball. After that, divide the dough into 8 equal pieces then roll each piece into worm like strips, about 9 inches long.

5. Tie each breadstick into a "knot-like" ball; place on the prepared baking sheet and spray the top with olive oil.

6. Bake on the top third of the oven until it turns golden for about 18 minutes. Let them cool for 5 minutes.

7. Meanwhile, in medium nonstick skillet melt the butter, add the garlic and cook until its golden for 2 minutes.

8. Toss the knots in the skillet with the melted butter and garlic or use a brush to cover the knots with the garlic.

9. If the knots are too dry, give them another mist of olive oil. Sprinkle with parmesan cheese and chopped parsley.

10. Serve immediately and enjoy.

Roasted Potatoes

Preparation time: 5 minutes

Cooking time: 24 minutes

Overall time: 29 minutes

Recipe Ingredients:

- ❖ 1.5 lb. potatoes (diced into 1-inch pieces)
- ❖ ½ tsp. of garlic powder or granulated garlic
- ❖ ½ tsp. of salt or more to taste
- ❖ ¼ tsp. of pepper
- ❖ ½ tsp. of oregano dried
- ❖ ½ tsp. of basil dried
- ❖ Cooking spray

Cooking Instructions:

1. Spray your Air-fryer cooking basket with the cooking spray. Then add diced potatoes to the basket, and give the potatoes a spray.

2. Add salt, pepper, garlic powder, oregano and basil, and toss thoroughly to combine well and evenly coat the potatoes.

3. Cook at 400ºF until it turns brown and crispy for about 20 to 24 minutes.

4. Toss them half way through with a flipper, and shake the basket once more to ensure even cooking.

5. Ready, serve and enjoy!

Brussels Sprouts with Bacon and Maple Syrup

Preparation time: 10 minutes

Cooking time: 15 minutes

Overall time: 25 minutes

Serves: 2 to 4

Recipe Ingredients:

* 1 lb. of brussels sprouts
* ¼ cup of olive or avocado oil
* ¼ cup of pure maple syrup
* 1 tbsp. of apple cider vinegar
* ½ tsp. of salt
* ¼ tsp. of pepper
* 4 bacon slices, (cut into ½-inch pieces)

Cooking Instructions:

1. Trim and halve the washed Brussels sprouts, removing discolored leaves. Larger sprouts may need to be quartered to keep sprouts uniform in size.

2. In a medium bowl, whisk together oil, maple syrup, vinegar, salt, and pepper thoroughly to combine well.

3. Add Brussels sprouts and raw bacon pieces to the bowl and gently stir to coat. Then spoon coated sprouts and bacon to the Air-fryer.

4. Cook at 350°F for about 10 to 15 minutes, until bacon and sprouts reach desired crispiness.

5. While cooking, open drawer halfway through cooking and stir contents.

6. Serve immediately!

APPETIZER RECIPES

Air-Fried Dill Pickle Fries with Ranch Breadcrumbs

Preparation time: 15 minutes

Cooking time: 10 minutes

Overall time: 25 Minutes

Serves: 4 to 8 people

Recipe Ingredients:

- ❖ 1 (16-oz.) drained jar of kosher dill pickle spears,
- ❖ ½ cup of all-purpose flour
- ❖ ¼ tsp. of black pepper
- ❖ ¾ cup of whole buttermilk
- ❖ 1 large egg
- ❖ 1 cup of panko
- ❖ 1 (1.4-oz.) envelope ranch dressing mix cooking spray
- ❖ 1 tbsp. of chopped fresh chives ranch dressing (optional)

Cooking Instructions:

1. Pat pickles very dry with paper towels. Then cut any spears that are too thick in half lengthwise to create ½-inch thick spears.

2. Combine flour and pepper in a shallow dish and whisk together buttermilk and egg in a second shallow dish.

3. Now stir together panko and ranch dressing mix in a third shallow dish. Dredge pickles in flour mixture, shaking off excess.

4. Dip in buttermilk mixture, and dredge in panko mixture, pressing it to coat evenly.

5. Working in batches, place pickles spears in a single layer in your air-fryer basket lightly coated with cooking spray.

6. Spray tops of pickles with cooking spray, if desired, for more browning and Cook at 400°F until it turn golden brown for about 8 to 10 minutes.

7. Repeat with remaining pickle spears. Sprinkle with chives, and serve with your favorite ranch dressing, if desired. Enjoy!

Jalapeño Poppers

Preparation time: 20 minutes

Cooking time: 24 minutes

Overall time: 44minutes

Serves: 2 to 4 people

Recipe Ingredients:

- ❖ 8 large jalapeño chiles
- ❖ 6 oz. cheddar cheese, shredded (about 1 ½ cups)
- ❖ 4 oz. cream cheese, softened
- ❖ 1 ½ tsp. of kosher salt, divided
- ❖ ½ cup of all-purpose flour
- ❖ 2 large eggs, beaten
- ❖ 1 ½ cups of panko
- ❖ ½ cup of sour cream
- ❖ ½ tsp. of lime zest, plus
- ❖ 2 tsp. of fresh lime juice

Cooking Instructions:

1. Bring 3 cups of water to a boil in a medium saucepan over high. Add jalapeños and cook, stirring occasionally for 3 minutes.

2. Transfer jalapeños to a bowl of ice water to stop the cooking process; let it stand for about 30 seconds.

3. Then transfer jalapeños to a plate lined with paper towels. Carefully make a slit vertically along the side of each jalapeño.

4. Wearing a glove, remove seeds and veins, after that rinse and dry thoroughly. After this process, stir together Cheddar, cream cheese, and ½ teaspoon of the salt in a medium bowl until combined.

5. Fill each pepper with about 2 teaspoons of cheese filling; close slit to seal in cheese. Place flour in 1 shallow dish, eggs in a second shallow dish, and panko and remaining 1 teaspoon salt in a third dish.

6. Dip stuffed jalapeños in eggs, allowing excess to drip off, then coat lightly in flour. Return coated jalapeños to egg dish for a second dip, and finally coat in panko.

7. Turn your Air-fryer to 375°F, and allow it to preheat for about 3 to 5 minutes. Now coat the basket and breaded jalapeños with cooking spray. Add 4 jalapeños at a time to Air-fryer.

8. Cook until it turns golden brown for about 10 to 12 minutes, turning half way through.

9. Repeat with remaining jalapeños. Combine sour cream, lime zest, and lime juice in a small bowl. Serve poppers with lime cream.

Shrimp Spring Rolls with Sweet Chili Sauce

Preparation time: 20 minutes

Cooking time: 35 minutes

Overall time: 55 minutes

Serves:2 to 4 people

Recipe Ingredients:

- 2 ½ tsp. of sesame oil, (divided)
- 2 cups of pre-shredded cabbage
- 1 cup of matchstick carrots
- 1 cup of julienne-cut red bell pepper
- 4 oz. of peeled, deveined raw shrimp, chopped
- ¾ cup of julienne-cut snow peas
- ¼ cup of chopped fresh cilantro
- 1 tbsp. of fresh lime juice
- 2 tsp. of fish sauce
- ¼ tsp. of crushed red pepper
- 8 (8-inch-square) of spring roll wrappers
- ½ cup of sweet chili sauce

Cooking Instructions:

1. Heat 1 ½ teaspoons of the oil in large skillet over high until slightly smoking.

2. Add cabbage, carrots, and bell pepper and cook while stirring constantly until it's lightly wilted, for about 1 to 1 ½ minutes.

3. Spread on a rimmed baking sheet; cool 5 minutes. Place cabbage mixture, shrimp, snow peas, cilantro, lime juice, fish sauce, and crushed red pepper in a large bowl and toss to combine.

4. Place spring roll wrappers on work surface with 1 corner facing you. Spoon ¼ cup of filling in center of each spring roll wrapper, spreading from left to right into a 3-inch long strip.

5. Fold bottom corner of each wrapper over filling, tucking tip of corner under filling.

6. Fold left and right corners over filling. Lightly brush remaining corner with water; tightly roll filled end toward remaining corner then gently press to seal.

7. Brush spring rolls with remaining 2 tablespoons oil. Place 4 spring rolls in air fryer basket, and cook at 390°F until its golden for about 6 to 7 minutes while turning spring rolls after 5 minutes.

8. Repeat with remaining spring rolls. Serve with sweet chili sauce and enjoy!

Mozzarella Sticks

Preparation time 10 minutes

Cooking time: 36 minutes

Overall time: 46 minutes

Serves: 2 to 4 people

Cooking Ingredients:

- ❖ 1 cup of all-purpose flour (about 4 ¼ oz.)
- ❖ 1 tsp. of baking soda
- ❖ 2 large eggs
- ❖ 1 tbsp. of whole milk
- ❖ 1 cup of seasoned panko
- ❖ 8 (1-oz.) mozzarella string cheese sticks
- ❖ ½ cup of marinara sauce

Cooking Instructions:

1. Combine flour and baking soda in a shallow dish. Whisk eggs and milk together in a second shallow dish, and pour panko in a third shallow dish.

2. Coat cheese sticks in flour mixture, and then in egg mixture; coat in breadcrumbs. Freeze breaded cheese sticks for about 30 minutes.

3. Lightly coat Air-fryer basket with cooking spray. Add 4 sticks at a time to fryer basket, and cook at 400°F for 6 minutes.

4. Repeat with remaining cheese sticks, and serve immediately with marinara sauce.

Air-Fried Buffalo Wings

Preparation time: 10 minutes

Cooking time: 1 hour 5 minutes

Overall time: 1 Hour 15 minutes

Serves: 2 to 4 people

Recipe Ingredients:

- ❖ 24 chicken wings
- ❖ 2 tsp. of kosher salt
- ❖ 1 tsp. of black pepper
- ❖ 1 tbsp. of cornstarch
- ❖ 1 cup of buffalo-style hot sauce

Cooking Instructions:

1. Place wings in an even layer on a baking sheet and pat wings dry with a paper towel. Then sprinkle evenly with salt, pepper and cornstarch, toss to coat.

2. Place 8 of the wings into your Air-fryer basket that has been lightly coated with cooking spray. After that, return basket to Air-fryer, set temperature to 400°F, and timer to 20 minutes.

3. Combine cooked wings and 1/3 cup of the buffalo sauce in a large bowl and flip to coat. Repeat process twice with remaining wings and sauce.

4. Serve and enjoy!

Crispy Sweet Potato Wedges

Preparation time: 10 minutes

Cooking time: 30 minutes

Serves: 2 to 3 people

Recipe Ingredients:

- ½ tsp. of paprika
- ¼ tsp. of ground cumin
- ¼ tsp. of black pepper
- 1/8 tsp. of kosher salt
- 1/8 tsp. of ground coriander
- 1/8 tsp. of garlic powder
- 1 (9-oz.) of sweet potato cut lengthwise into 8 wedges
- 1 tsp. of canola oil
- 1 tbsp. of fresh cilantro leaves
- 2 lime wedges

Cooking Instructions:

1. Mix-up paprika, cumin, pepper, salt, coriander, and garlic powder in a small bowl and stir thoroughly.

2. Toss potato wedges with oil in a medium bowl and sprinkle with spice mixture.

3. Place potatoes in Air-fryer basket, and cook at 400°F for 20 minutes or until it becomes very crispy, turning potato wedges over halfway through cooking.

4. Transfer to a bowl, and sprinkle with cilantro. Serve and enjoy with lime wedges.

Coconut Shrimp

Preparation time: 15 minutes

Cooking time: 30 minutes

Overall time: 45 minutes

Serves 4 people

Recipe Ingredients:

- ½ cup (2 1/8 oz.) of all-purpose flour
- 1 ½ teaspoons black pepper
- 2 large eggs
- 2/3 cup of unsweetened flaked coconut
- 1/3 cup of panko
- 12 oz. of medium peeled, deveined raw shrimp, tail-on
- Cooking spray
- ½ tsp. kosher salt
- 1/4 cup of honey
- 1/4 cup of lime juice
- 1 Serrano Chile, thinly sliced (2 teaspoons chopped fresh cilantro)-optional

Cooking Instructions:

1. Mix-up flour and pepper in a shallow dish and stir to combine well. Then lightly beat eggs in a second shallow dish.

2. Whisk together coconut and panko in a third shallow dish. Holding each shrimp by the tail, dredge shrimp in flour mixture, making sure not to coat tail and shake off excess after coating.

3. Dip in egg, while allowing any excess to drip off, dredge in coconut mixture and , press it to adhere. Coat shrimp well with cooking spray.

4. Place half of the shrimp in Air-fryer basket, and cook for about 6 to 8 minutes at 400°F until it turns golden.

5. Turn shrimp over halfway through cooking and season with ¼ teaspoon of the salt. Repeat with remaining shrimp and salt.

6. While shrimp cook, whisk together honey, lime juice, and serrano chile in small bowl. Sprinkle shrimp with cilantro, if desired and serve with sauce.

Buffalo Cauliflower Bites

Preparation time: 10 minutes

Cooking time: 40 minutes

Overall time: 50 minutes

Serves: 4 to 5 people

Recipe Ingredients:

- 3 tbsp. of no-salt-added ketchup
- 2 tbsp. of hot sauce
- 1 large egg white
- 3/4 cup panko
- ½ (3 pounds) head cauliflower, trimmed and cut into 1-inch florets
- ¼ cup of reduced-fat sour cream
- ¼ ounce crumbled blue cheese
- 1 small garlic clove, grated
- 1 tsp. of red wine vinegar
- ¼ tsp. of black pepper

Cooking Instructions:

1. Whisk together ketchup, hot sauce, and egg white in a small bowl until its smooth.

2. Place panko in a large bowl and toss together cauliflower florets and ketchup mixture in a second large bowl until it's coated.

3. While working in batches, toss cauliflower in panko to coat and coat cauliflower well with cooking spray.

4. Place half of the cauliflower in Air-fryer basket, and cook for about 20 minutes at 320°F until its golden brown and crispy, repeat with remaining cauliflower.

5. While cauliflower cooks, stir together sour cream, blue cheese, garlic, vinegar, and pepper in small bowl. Serve and enjoy cauliflower with blue cheese sauce.

"Everything Bagel" Kale Chips

Preparation time: 10 minutes

Cooking time: 10 minutes

Overall time: 20 minutes

Serves: 2 people

Recipe Ingredients:

- ❖ 6 cups of packed torn lacinato kale leaves, (stems and ribs removed)
- ❖ 1 tbsp. of olive oil
- ❖ 1 tsp. of lower-sodium soy sauce
- ❖ 1 tsp. of white or black sesame seeds
- ❖ ½ tsp. of dried minced garlic
- ❖ ¼ tsp. of poppy seeds

Cooking Instructions:

1. Wash and completely dry kale leaves, and tear it into 1 ½-inch pieces.

2. Toss together kale, olive oil, and soy sauce in a medium sized bowl, rubbing the leaves gently to be sure they are well coated with mixture.

3. Place one-third of the kale leaves in Air-fryer basket, and cook for about 6 minutes at 375°F until it's crispy while shaking basket halfway through cooking.

4. Place kale chips on a baking sheet, and sprinkle evenly with sesame seeds, garlic, and poppy seeds while still hot. Repeat with remaining kale leaves.

5. Serve immediately and enjoy!

Curry Chickpeas

Preparation time: 10 minutes

Cooking time: 15 minutes

Overall time: 25 minutes

Serves:2 to 4 people

Recipe Ingredients:

- ❖ 1 (15 ounces.) can of no-salt-added chickpeas, drained and rinsed
- ❖ 2 tbsp. of red wine vinegar
- ❖ 2 tbsp. of olive oil
- ❖ 2 tsp. of curry powder
- ❖ 1/2 tsp. of ground turmeric
- ❖ ¼ tsp. of ground coriander
- ❖ ¼ tsp. of ground cumin
- ❖ ¼ tsp. of plus
- ❖ 1/8 tsp. of ground cinnamon
- ❖ ¼ tsp. of kosher salt
- ❖ ½ tsp. of thinly sliced fresh cilantro aleppo pepper

Cooking Instructions:

1. Tenderly smash chickpeas with your hands in a medium bowl (do not crush) and discard chickpea skins.

2. Add vinegar and oil to chickpeas, and toss to coat. Add curry powder, turmeric, coriander, cumin, and cinnamon and stir gently to combine.

3. Place chickpeas in single layer in Air-fryer basket, and cook for about 15 minutes at 400°F until it becomes crispy while shaking chickpeas halfway through cooking.

4. Transfer chickpeas to a bowl and sprinkle with salt, Aleppo pepper, and cilantro, and then toss to coat.

5. Serve immediately and enjoy!

Crispy, Sweet Air-Fried Beet Chips

Preparation time: 15 minutes

Cooking time: 30 minutes

Overall time: 45 minutes

Serves: 2 to 4 people

Recipe Ingredients:

- ❖ 3 medium-size red beets, peeled and cut into 1/8-inch-thick slices
- ❖ 2 tsp. of canola oil
- ❖ ¾ tsp. of kosher salt
- ❖ ¼ tsp. of black pepper

Cooking Instructions:

1. Toss sliced beets, oil, salt, and pepper in a large bowl.

2. Then place half of the beets in air fryer basket, and cook for about 25 to 30 minutes at 320°F until dry and crisp.

3. Shake the basket every 5 minutes through cooking. Repeat with remaining beets.

4. Serve immediately and enjoy!

FISH AND SEAFOOD RECIPES
Fish Sticks
Preparation time: 15 minutes

Cooking time: 12 minutes

Overall time: 27 minutes

Recipe Ingredients:

- ❖ 4 (4 ounces) fillets of frozen cod or tilapia thawed
- ❖ ¼ cup of whole wheat flour
- ❖ 1 tsp. of paprika
- ❖ 1 tsp. of garlic powder
- ❖ 1 tsp. of salt plus more for sprinkling after air frying
- ❖ ½ tsp. of pepper
- ❖ 2 large eggs
- ❖ 1 large lemon juiced, plus more for serving after air frying
- ❖ 1 cup of panko breadcrumbs
- ❖ 2 tsp. of old bay
- ❖ Tarter sauce (recommended for serving)

Cooking Instructions:

1. Firstly, on your Air-fryer. Then preheat at 400ºF and set the timer to 10 to 12 minutes.

2. Then press "Start", the Air-fryer will beep at you when it's finished preheating.

3. Once preheated, spray the basket with cooking spray and place in approximately 6 pieces of fish and make sure they aren't touching.

4. After 5 minutes, carefully flip each piece of fish, and then continue cooking for the remaining 5 minutes.

5. Remove from Air-fryer, sprinkle with more salt (if necessary) and a generous squeeze of lemon. Repeat with remaining fish. Serve and enjoy with tarter sauce!

Crispy Fish Tacos with Slaw

Preparation time: 15 minutes

Cooking time: 18 minutes

Overall time: 33 minutes

Serves: 2 to 4 people

Recipe Ingredients:

- ❖ 1 serving nonstick of cooking spray
- ❖ 4 cups of cabbage slaw mix
- ❖ 1 tbsp. of chopped fresh jalapeno pepper
- ❖ 1 tbsp. of lime juice
- ❖ 1 tbsp. of olive oil
- ❖ 1 tbsp. of apple cider vinegar
- ❖ ½ tsp. of salt
- ❖ ¼ tsp. of ground black pepper
- ❖ ¼ tsp. of ground cayenne pepper
- ❖ ¼ cup of all-purpose flour
- ❖ ¼ cup of yellow cornmeal
- ❖ 2 tbsp. of taco seasoning mix
- ❖ 1 pound of cod fillets, cut into bite-sized pieces
- ❖ 8 (6 inch) corn tortillas

Cooking Instructions:

1. Preheat an air fryer to 400º F and spray the basket of the Air-fryer with cooking spray.

2. Combine cabbage slaw, jalapeno pepper, lime juice, olive oil, vinegar, salt, pepper, and cayenne pepper in a large bowl. Then mix until evenly combined and set it aside.

3. Mix together flour, cornmeal, and taco seasoning in a separate bowl. Add fish pieces and toss until evenly coated, discarding any remaining seasoning mix.

4. Place in the prepared Air-fryer basket and mist lightly with cooking spray.

5. Cook fish in the preheated air fryer for 5 minutes and shake the basket, then cook until fish is crispy and flakes easily with a fork, for about 5 minutes more.

6. Remove to a paper towel-lined plate. Place cabbage slaw mixture into the Air-fryer basket and cook until cabbage is caramelized, for about 8 minutes, stirring halfway through the cooking time. Spoon cabbage onto tortillas and top with fish.

Tilapia

Preparation time: 15 minutes

Cooking time: 5 minutes

Overall time: 20 minutes

Serves: 2 to 4 people

Recipe Ingredients:

- ❖ 4 fillets of tilapia
- ❖ ½ cup of flour
- ❖ 4 oz. of parmesan cheese, grated
- ❖ 2 tsp. of lemon zest
- ❖ 1 tsp. of salt
- ❖ 1 tsp. of garlic powder
- ❖ ½ tsp. of black pepper
- ❖ ½ tsp. of paprika
- ❖ 2 eggs

Cooking Instructions:

1. Place 3 shallow dishes and put the flour in another dish. Crack the egg into another dish and whisk the eggs thoroughly.

2. In the third dish, mix-up the cheese, paprika, lemon zest, salt and pepper and combine well.

3. Pat the tilapia fillets dry then dip each fillet into the flour and coat both sides. Dip them into the egg wash and transfer them to the cheese mixture to coat both sides of each fillet.

4. Place a small piece of parchment paper on the bottom of the Air-fryer basket then place 1 to 2 fillets in the basket.

5. Cook for about 4 to 5 minutes at 400°F until the cheese melts and the crust is golden brown. Serve immediately and enjoy!

Healthy White Fish with Garlic and Lemon

Preparation time: 5 minutes

Cooking time: 12 minutes

Over all time: 17 minutes

Serves: 2 to 4 people

Recipe Ingredients:

- ❖ 12 oz. of tilapia filets or 2 filets (6 oz. each)
- ❖ ½ tsp. of garlic powder (2.5 ml)
- ❖ ½ tsp. of lemon pepper seasoning (2.5 ml)
- ❖ ½ tsp. of onion powder (optional)
- ❖ Kosher salt or sea salt , to taste
- ❖ Fresh cracked black pepper , to taste
- ❖ Fresh chopped parsley
- ❖ Lemon wedges

Cooking Instructions:

1. Pre-heat your Air-fryer at 360°F for 5 minutes. Rinse and pat dry the fish filets.

2. Spray or coat with olive oil spray and season with garlic powder, lemon pepper, and/or onion powder, salt and pepper. Repeat for both sides.

3. Lay perforated Air-fryer baking paper inside base of air fryer and lightly spray the paper.

4. If you are not using a liner, spray enough olive oil spray at the base of the Air-fryer basket to make sure fish does not stick.

5. Lay the fish on top of the paper and add a few lemon wedges next to fish. Line with Parchment Paper.

6. After that, Air-Fry at 360°F for about 6 to12 minutes, or until fish can be flaked with a fork.

7. Timing will depend on how thickness of the filets, how cold the filets are, and individual preference.

8. Sprinkle with chopped parsley and serve warm with the toasted lemon wedges.

Fish and Chips

Preparation time: 5 minutes

Cooking time: 10 minutes

Overall time: 15 minutes

Serves: 2 to 4 people

Recipe Ingredients:

- ❖ 1 lb. of cod fillet cut into strips
- ❖ ½ cup of all-purpose flour
- ❖ 2 tsp. paprika
- ❖ ½ tsp. of garlic powder
- ❖ ¼ tsp. of salt
- ❖ ¼ tsp. of black pepper
- ❖ Large egg beaten
- ❖ 2 cups of panko breadcrumbs
- ❖ Tartar sauce for serving
- ❖ Lemon wedges for serving

Cooking Instructions:

1. Mix-up flour with the paprika, garlic powder and salt in a small bowl. Place the beaten egg in another bowl and the panko breadcrumbs in a third bowl.

2. Pat the fish dry using a paper towel. After that, dredge the fish in the flour mixture, then the egg and finally the panko breadcrumbs.

3. Press it down lightly until the crumbs sticks. Then spray both sides with oil.

4. Now Air-fry at 400ºF for about for 10 to 12 minutes, turning halfway through cooking until it's crispy and lightly golden.

5. Open basket and check for desired doneness with a fork to see if it flakes off easily. Return the fish for another 1 or 2 minutes if necessary.

6. Serve immediately with fries and tartar sauce, and enjoy!

Zesty Ranch Fish Fillets

Preparation time: 5 minutes

Cooking time: 12 minutes

Overall time: 17 minutes

Serves: 2 to 4 people

Recipe Ingredients:

- ❖ ¾ cup of bread crumbs or panko
- ❖ 130g packet of dry ranch-style dressing mix
- ❖ 2 ½ tbsp. of vegetable oil
- ❖ 2 eggs beaten
- ❖ 4 tilapia salmon or other fish fillets
- ❖ Lemon wedges to garnish

Cooking Instructions:

1. Preheat your Air-fryer at 180ºC.Mix the panko/breadcrumbs and the ranch dressing mix together.

2. Add in the oil and keep stirring until the mixture becomes loose and crumbly.

3. After that, dip the fish fillets into the egg, letting the excess drip off, dip the fish fillets into the crumb mixture, making sure they are coated evenly and thoroughly.

4. Now place fish fillets into your Air-fryer carefully and cook for 12 to 13 minutes, depending on the thickness of the fillets.

5. Remove and serve immediately. Squeeze the lemon wedges over the fish if desired.

Southern Fried Catfish Nuggets

Preparation time: 5 minutes

Cooking time: 17 minutes

Overall time: 22 minutes

Recipe Ingredients:

- ❖ 2 pounds of catfish nuggets
- ❖ ¼ cup of oil
- ❖ 10 ounces box of fish fry mix

Cooking Instructions:

1. Firstly, rinse fish and set aside. Pour half the box of fish fry mix into a large Ziploc bag.

2. Add the Catfish Nuggets a few at a time into the bag with the fish fry mix. Seal the bag and shake well to coat.

3. Using the tongs, remove the nuggets one at a time, shaking off excess batter.

4. Add the catfish nuggets to the basket of the Air-fryer. Check the directions of your Air-fryer for filling the basket in case it requires no over filling of basket.

5. Pour the oil into a small bowl, dip your basting brush into the oil and baste a small amount of oil onto the top of each catfish nugget.

6. Set your Air-fryer on to 380°F and set timer for 17 minutes. Start checking at about 12 minutes because Air-fryers do not cook the exact same and don't not shake while cooking.

7. Remove from basket when done and drain on paper toweling. Add the next batch to the basket and repeat.

8. Total cooking time will depend on how many batches you do. Serve when ready and enjoy!

Beer Battered Fish

Preparation time: 10 minutes

Cooking time: 12 minutes

Resting time: 20 minutes

Overall time: 42 minutes

Serves: 5 people

Recipe Ingredients:

* 1 cup of all-purpose flour
* 2 tbsp. of cornstarch
* ½ tsp. of baking soda
* 6 oz. of beer
* 1 egg beaten
* ¾ cup of all-purpose flour
* ½ tsp. of paprika
* 1 tsp. of salt
* ¼ tsp. of freshly ground black pepper
* Pinch of cayenne pepper
* 1½ lb. of cod cut into 4 or 5 pieces
* Vegetable oil

Cooking Instructions:

1. Combine the 1 cup of flour, cornstarch and baking soda in a large bowl and add the beer and egg, stir until it's smooth. Cover the bowl of batter with plastic wrap and refrigerate for at least 20 minutes.

2. Combine the ¾ cup of flour, paprika, salt, black pepper and cayenne pepper in a shallow dredging pan.

3. Pat the cod fish fillets dry with a paper towel. Now dip the fish into the batter, coating all sides and allow the excess batter to drip off and then coat each fillet with the seasoned flour.

4. Sprinkle any leftover flour on the fish fillets and pat gently to adhere the flour to the batter. After that, pre-heat your air fryer at 390°F.

5. Generously spritz both sides of the coated fish filets with vegetable oil and place them in the Air-fryer basket.

6. Air-fry for 12 minutes at 390°F. Then spritz with more oil during the cooking process if there are any dry spots on the coating. Serve immediately with lemon wedges, malt vinegar and tartar sauce.

Breaded Sea Scallops

Preparation time: 10 minutes

Cooking time: 5 minutes

Overall time: 15 minutes

Serves: 2 to 4 people

Recipe Ingredients:

- ❖ ½ cup of finely crushed buttery crackers
- ❖ ½ tsp. of garlic powder
- ❖ ½ tsp. of seafood seasoning
- ❖ 2 tbsp. of butter, melted
- ❖ 1 lb. of sea scallops, patted dry
- ❖ 1 serving cooking spray

Cooking Instructions:

1. Preheat the Air-fryer to 390°F. Mix cracker crumbs, garlic powder, and seafood seasoning together in a shallow bowl.

2. Place melted butter in a second shallow bowl. Then start to dip each scallop in the melted butter and roll in the breading until it's completely coated.

3. Set on a plate and repeat with the remaining scallops. Lightly spray the air fryer basket with cooking spray.

4. Arrange scallops in the prepared basket so that they don't touching each other. You may require working in batches.

5. Cook in the preheated air-fryer for 2 minutes. Turn scallops over gently with a small spatula and cook until it's opaque for about 2 more minutes.

Crumbed Fish

Preparation: 10 minutes

Cooking time: 12 minutes

Overall time: 22 minutes

Serves: 2 to 4 people

Recipe Ingredients:

- ❖ 1 cup of dry bread crumbs
- ❖ ¼ cup of vegetable oil
- ❖ 4 eaches of flounder fillets
- ❖ 1 egg, beaten
- ❖ 1 sliced lemon

Cooking Instructions:

1. Preheat your Air-fryer at 350ºF in a bowl, mix bread crumbs and oil together and stir until mixture becomes loose and crumbly.

2. Dip fish fillets into the egg; shake off any excess. Dip fillets into the bread crumb mixture; coat evenly and fully.

3. Lay coated fillets gently in the preheated air fryer and cook for about 12 minutes until fish flakes easily with a fork. Garnish with lemon slices.

4. Serve and enjoy!

Cajun Salmon

Preparation time: 10 minutes

Cooking time: 10 minutes

Overall time: 20 minutes

Serves: 2 people

Recipe Ingredients:

- ❖ 6 oz. of skin-on salmon fillets
- ❖ 1 serving cooking spray
- ❖ 1 tbsp. of Cajun seasoning
- ❖ 1 tsp. of brown sugar

Cooking Instructions:

1. Preheat the Air-fryer to 390ºF. Rinse and dry salmon fillets with a paper towel.

2. Mist fillets with cooking spray and combine Cajun seasoning and brown sugar in a small bowl.

3. Sprinkle onto a plate and press flesh sides of fillets into the seasoning mixture.

4. Spray the basket of the Air-fryer with cooking spray and place salmon fillets skin-side down. Mist salmon again lightly with cooking spray.

5. Cook for 8 minutes then remove from Air-fryer and let rest for 2 minutes before serving.

6. Serve and enjoy!

Crab Cakes

Preparation time: 15 minutes
Cooking time: 10 minutes
Extra time: 1 hour
Overall time: 1 hour 25 minutes
Serves: 4 to 5 people

Cooking Ingredients:

- ❖ 1 large egg, beaten
- ❖ 2 tbsp. of mayonnaise
- ❖ 1 tsp. of worcestershire sauce
- ❖ 1 tsp. of dijon mustard
- ❖ 1 tsp. of seafood seasoning
- ❖ ½ tsp. of hot pepper sauce
- ❖ 2 tbsp. of finely chopped green onion
- ❖ 1 lb. of lump crabmeat, drained and picked over
- ❖ 3 tbsp. of milk
- ❖ 1 pinch of salt and ground black pepper to taste
- ❖ 11 crackers saltine crackers, crushed
- ❖ 1 tsp. of baking powder
- ❖ 4 wedges lemon
- ❖ 1 serving olive oil cooking spray

Cooking Instructions:

1. Mix-up egg, mayonnaise, Worcestershire sauce, mustard, seafood seasoning, and hot pepper sauce in a small mixing bowl and stir in green onion and set aside.

2. Place crab meat in a medium bowl and break up with a fork. Then add milk, salt, and pepper and toss to coat.

3. Add crushed saltines and baking powder and toss lightly to combine. Add to the egg mixture, stirring gently and being careful not to break apart the crab lumps.

4. Scoop crab with a 1/3-cup measure and form into 8 patties. Place patties on a plate, cover, and refrigerate for about 1 hour or until its firm.

5. Preheat your Air-fryer at 400ºF then spray crab cakes on both sides with cooking spray and place them in the air fryer basket.

6. Cook for 5 minutes, then gently turn the cakes over, and cook 5 minutes longer until it turns crispy brown. Serve immediately!

Lemon Pepper Shrimp

Preparation time: 5 minutes

Cooking time: 10 minutes

Overall time: 15 minutes

Serves: 2 to 4 people

Recipe Ingredients:

- ❖ 1 tbsp. of olive oil
- ❖ 1 lemon, juiced
- ❖ 1 tsp. of lemon pepper
- ❖ ¼ tsp. of paprika
- ❖ ¼ tsp. of garlic powder
- ❖ 12 oz. of uncooked medium shrimp, peeled and deveined
- ❖ 1 Lemon, sliced

Cooking Instructions:

1. Preheat your Air-fryer to 400ºF. Then mix olive oil, lemon juice, lemon pepper, paprika, and garlic powder in a bowl. Add shrimp and toss until it's coated.

2. Place shrimp in the air fryer and cook until it turns pink and firm for about 6 to 10 minutes.

3. Serve with lemon slices.

Lobster Tails with Lemon-Garlic Butter

Preparation time: 10 minutes

Cooking time: 10 minutes

Cooking time: 20 minutes

Serves: 2 to 4 people

Cooking Ingredients:

- ❖ 4 oz. of lobster tails
- ❖ 4 tbsp. of butter
- ❖ 1 tsp. of lemon zest
- ❖ 1 clove of garlic, grated
- ❖ 1 pinch of salt and ground black pepper to taste
- ❖ 1 tsp. of chopped fresh parsley
- ❖ 2 wedges lemon

Cooking Instructions:

1. Butterfly lobster tails by cutting lengthwise through the centers of the hard top shells and meat with kitchen shears.

2. Cut to, but not through, the bottoms of the shells. Spread the tail halves apart.

3. Then place tails in the Air-fryer basket with lobster meat facing up. Melt butter in a small saucepan over medium heat.

4. Add lemon zest and garlic and heat until garlic is tender for about 30 seconds.

5. Transfer 2 tablespoons of butter mixture to a small bowl and brush onto lobster tails, discard any remaining brushed butter to avoid contamination from uncooked lobster.

6. Season lobster with salt and pepper then cook for 5 to 7 minutes in an air fryer at 380ºF until lobster meat is opaque.

7. Spoon reserved butter from the saucepan over lobster meat. Top with parsley and serve with lemon wedges.

VEGETERIAN RECIEPES

Avocado Egg Rolls with Sweet Chili Sauce

Preparation time: 20 minutes

Cooking time: 25 minutes

Overall time: 45 minutes

Serves: 5 to 6 people

Recipe Ingredients:

- ❖ 10 egg roll wrappers
- ❖ 3 avocados peeled and pitted
- ❖ 1 diced roma tomato
- ❖ ½ tsp. of salt
- ❖ ¼ tsp. of pepper
- ❖ Canola oil for frying

For sweet chili sauce:

- ❖ 4 tbsp. of sriracha
- ❖ 2 tbsp. of white sugar
- ❖ 1 tbsp. of rice vinegar
- ❖ 1 tbsp. of sesame oil

Cooking Instructions:

1. In a mixing bowl, add avocados, tomato, salt, and pepper and stir. Squash the avocados to a chunky consistency and stir to combine the ingredients.

2. This will become the egg roll filling. Lay out the egg roll wrappers and a small bowl of water.

3. Distribute the egg roll filling among the wrappers, scooping them onto the bottom third of each wrapper.

4. Taking one wrapper at a time, use a finger to brush water along its four edges. Then fold up a corner over the filling, the sides, and then roll it up.

5. Pat the last fold with more water to seal, then repeat for all other wrappers.

6. Add canola oil to a large pot until the oil is about 2 inches deep. Turn the burner to medium heat.

7. When the oil temperature reaches 350ºF, add the egg rolls in batches and cook until it turns golden brown for about 3 minutes.

8. Transfer to a paper towel to drain, and then slice each egg roll diagonally. Combine sauce ingredients in a small bowl and mix thoroughly.

9. Serve with sliced avocado egg rolls.

Buffalo Cauliflower

Preparation time: 8 minutes

Cooking time: 14 minutes

Overall time: 22 minutes

Serves: 3 to 4 people

Recipe Ingredients:

- 1 medium head cauliflower (chopped into 1 ½ florets)
- 2 to 3 tbsp. of frank's red hot sauce
- 1 ½ tsp. of maple syrup
- 2 tsp. of avocado oil
- 2 to 3 tablespoons nutritional yeast
- ¼ tsp. of sea salt
- 1 tbsp. of cornstarch or arrowroot starch

Cooking Instructions:

1. Set your Air-fryer to 360ºF and add all ingredients except cauliflower to a large mixing bowl.

2. Whisk to combine thoroughly then add cauliflower and toss to coat uniformly.

3. Add half of your cauliflower to Air-fryer and cook for 12 to 14 minutes, shaking halfway, or until you reach desired evenness.

4. Repeat with remaining cauliflower and set lower cook time to 9 to 10 minutes.

5. Keep Cauliflower tightly sealed in the refrigerator for about 4 days. Then to reheat, put back Cauliflower to Air-fryer for 1 to 2 minutes, until it's warmed through and slightly crispy.

6. Serve immediately and enjoy!

Vegan Fried Ravioli

Preparation time: 15 minutes

Cooking time: 8 minutes

Overall time: 23 minutes

Recipe Ingredients

- ½ cup of panko bread crumbs
- 2 tsp. of nutritional yeast flakes
- 1 tsp. of dried basil
- 1 tsp. of dried oregano
- 1 tsp. of garlic powder
- Pinch of salt and pepper
- ¼ cup of aquafaba liquid (from can of chickpeas or other beans)
- 8 oz. of frozen or thawed vegan ravioli**
- Spritz cooking spray
- ½ cup of marinara for dipping

Cooking Instructions:

1. In a mixing plate, combine panko bread crumbs, nutritional yeast flakes, dried basil, dried oregano, garlic powder, salt, and pepper.

2. Place aquafaba into a small separate bowl, dip ravioli into aquafaba, shake off excess liquid, and then dredge in bread crumb mixture.

3. Make sure that the ravioli gets fully covered then move the ravioli into the air fryer basket.

4. Continue until all of the ravioli has been breaded. Be careful not to overlap the ravioli too much in the Air-fryer, so that they can brown evenly. You may need to, air-fry in batches.

5. Spritz the ravioli with cooking spray and set air fryer to 390°F. after that, Air-fry for 6 minutes,

6. Then carefully flip each ravioli over. Don't shake the basket so that you won't lose a lot of bread crumbs. Air-fry for 2 more minutes.

7. Remove ravioli from Air-fryer and serve with warm marinara for dipping.

Vegan Cheese Samboosa

Preparation time: 30 minutes

Cooking time: 12 minutes

Overall time: 42 minutes

Serves: 15 to 20 people

Recipe Ingredients:

For the Cheese

- ❖ ½ cup of raw cashews (pre-boiled for 10 minutes)
- ❖ 3 tablespoons of nutritional yeast
- ❖ 3 tablespoons +2 teaspoons of tapioca starch
- ❖ ¾ teaspoon of sea salt
- ❖ 1 teaspoon of apple cider vinegar
- ❖ 1¼ cup of water

For the Samboosa

- ❖ 1 package of samosa pastry sheets
- ❖ 1 tablespoon of olive oil
- ❖ ½ cup of water

Cooking Instructions:

1. Add all the cheese ingredients to a blender and blend on high until it becomes smooth.

2. Pour the blended mixture into a small saucepan on medium heat, then using a wooden spoon or spatula, stir continuously while cooking.

3. You will see small clumps that will start to form, as you do and at about 5 minute, your mixture should turn into one big gooey mass of cheese.

4. Cook for an additional 30 seconds to one minute to ensure everything is firmed up.

5. Store in a glass container and allow it to cool in the fridge for at least 30 minutes before handling.

6. To assemble, place a samosa pastry sheet vertically on a cutting board or plate and start by adding a light wash of water using a pastry brush.

7. Add about 1 to 2 teaspoons of the cheese mixture to the far right corner, then using the bottom right "point" fold the pastry over the filling in a triangle shape.

8. After that, take the top right point of that triangle and fold horizontally, alternating the previous two steps until you have a triangle shaped parcel, sealing down the final flap.

9. Go on until all samosa sheets are used up. Brush each samboosa lightly with olive oil on each side.

10. Then place 4 to 6 parcels at a time in your Air-fryer basket and cook on 200ºC for 6 to 10 minutes until it is slightly browned and crispy.

11. Serve immediately while you enjoy!

Garlic and Herb Air-Fryer Roasted Chickpeas

Preparation time: 5 minutes

Cooking time: 20 minutes

Overall time: 25 minutes

Serves: Serves 4 to 5 people

Recipe Ingredients:

- ❖ 2 cans of chickpeas
- ❖ 1 tablespoon of olive oil
- ❖ 1 tablespoon of nutritional yeast
- ❖ 2 tablespoons of garlic powder
- ❖ 1 tablespoon of mixed herbs
- ❖ Sea salt and black pepper to taste

Cooking Instructions:

1. Drain and rinse the chickpeas, then add to a medium-sized mixing bowl and add in the olive oil and seasonings.

2. Stir thoroughly well to combine using a spatula, ensuring all chickpeas are well coated.

3. Divide and cook in two batches in the air-fryer at 200°C for 15 to 20 minutes, stirring once at the 10 minute mark.

4. While cooking, you may hear some popping sound which is totally normal. Once they are golden brown and crispy, they're done all the way through.

5. Serve while warm and store in an air-tight jar once cooled to preserve crispiness.

Thai Veggie Bites

Preparation time: 5 minutes

Cooking time: 45minutes

Resting time: 1 hour

Overall time: 1 hour 50 minutes

Serves: 10 to 15 people

Recipe Ingredients:

- 1 large broccoli
- 1 large cauliflower
- 6 large carrots
- Handful garden peas
- ½ cauliflower made into cauliflower rice
- 1 large peeled and diced onion
- 1 small courgette
- 2 leeks cleaned and thinly sliced
- 1 can of coconut milk
- 50 g plain flour
- 1(cm) cube ginger peeled and grated
- 1 tablespoon of garlic puree
- 1 tablespoon of olive oil
- 1 tablespoon of thai green curry paste
- 1 tablespoon of coriander
- 1 tablespoon of mixed spice
- 1 teaspoon of cumin
- Salt and pepper

Cooking Instructions:

1. In a wok, cook your onion with the garlic, ginger and olive oil until the onion has a good bit of colour on it.

2. While you are cooking your onion in a steamer, cook your vegetables except the courgette and leek for 20 minutes or until they are almost cooked.

3. Then add the courgette, the leek and the curry paste to your wok and cook on a medium heat for more 5 minutes.

4. Add the coconut milk and the rest of the seasoning combine very well and then add the cauliflower rice. After that, mix again and allow boiling for 10 minutes.

5. Once it has boiled for 10 minutes and the sauce has reduced by half, add the steamed vegetables.

6. Combine well and you will now have a lovely base for your veggie bites. Place in the fridge for an hour to allow it cool.

7. After an hour make into bite sizes and place in the Air Fryer. Cook for 10 minutes at 180°C and then serve with a cooling dip.

Classic Falafel

Serves: 8 people

Recipe Ingredients:

- ❖ 1 ½ cups of dry garbanzo beans
- ❖ ½ cup of chopped fresh parsley
- ❖ ½ cup of chopped fresh cilantro
- ❖ ½ cup of chopped white onion
- ❖ 7 cloves of garlic
- ❖ 2 tablespoons of all-purpose flour
- ❖ ½ teaspoon of sea salt
- ❖ 1 tablespoon of ground cumin
- ❖ ⅛ teaspoon of ground cardamom
- ❖ 1 teaspoon of ground coriander
- ❖ ⅛ teaspoon of cayenne pepper

Cooking Instructions:

1. Place dried garbanzo beans in a large bowl and cover with 1 inch of water and soak overnight.

2. Let it sit, uncovered, for 20 to 24 hours and drain thoroughly. Rinse garbanzo beans in a strainer and add to a large pot.

3. Cover it with 2 inches of water and bring to a boil for 1 minute. After 1 minute, cover pot and remove from heat letting it stand for 1 hour, and then you drain thoroughly.

4. Add parsley, cilantro, onion and garlicin in the bowl of a food processor and mix until it is well combined.

5. Now add soaked garbanzo beans, flour, salt, cumin, cardamom, coriander and cayenne to food processor.

6. Pulse until ingredients form a rough, coarse meal. Scrape down sides of food processor occasionally.

7. Place mixture into a bowl, cover and refrigerate for 1 to 2 hours to allow flavors to come together.

8. Once cooled, remove from refrigerator and form it into 1½-inch balls, then flatten balls slightly to form patties.

9. Preheat air fryer to 400°F and lightly spray fryer basket with oil. Then place falafel into basket, being careful not to overcrowd.

10. Cook for 10 minutes, turning halfway through cooking. Repeat with remaining falafel.

11. Serve immediately and enjoy!

Cauliflower Chickpea Tacos

Preparation time: 10 minutes

Cooking time: 20 minutes

Overall time: 30 minutes

Serves: 2 to 4 people

Recipe Ingredients:

- ❖ 4 cups of cauliflower florets cut into bite sized pieces
- ❖ 19 ounces of can of chickpeas drained and rinsed
- ❖ 2 tbsp. of olive oil
- ❖ 2 tbsp. of taco seasoning
- ❖ 8 small tortillas
- ❖ 2 sliced avocados
- ❖ 4 cups of cabbage shredded
- ❖ Coconut yogurt to drizzle

Cooking Instructions:

1. Pre-heat your Air-fryer to 390°F. Then in a large bowl, toss the cauliflower and chickpeas with the olive oil and taco seasoning.

2. Dump everything into the basket of your Air-fryer and cook in the Air-fryer, shaking the basket occasionally for 20 minutes or until cauliflower becomes golden but not burnt.

3. Serve in tacos with avocado slices, cabbage and coconut yogurt.

Kale and Potato Nuggets

Serves: 2 to 4 people

Recipe Ingredients:

- ❖ 2 cups of finely chopped potatoes
- ❖ 1 tsp. of extra-virgin olive oil or canola oil
- ❖ 1 minced clove garlic
- ❖ 4 cups of loosely packed coarsely chopped kale
- ❖ 1/8 cup of almond milk
- ❖ ¼ tsp. of sea salt
- ❖ 1/8 tsp. of ground black pepper
- ❖ Vegetable oil spray as needed

Cooking Instructions:

1. Put in the potatoes to a large saucepan of boiling water and cook until it becomes tender for about 30 minutes.

2. In a large skillet, heat the oil over medium-high heat. Then add the garlic and sauté until it becomes golden brown.

3. Add the kale and sauté for 2 to 3 minutes and transfer to a large bowl. After that, drain the cooked potatoes and transfer them to a medium bowl.

4. Add the milk, salt, and pepper and mash with a fork or potato masher. Transfer the potatoes to a large bowl and combine with the cooked kale.

5. Preheat your air fryer at 390°F for 5 minutes and then roll the potato and kale mixture into 1-inch nuggets.

6. Spritz the air fryer basket with vegetable oil, place the nuggets in the Air-fryer and cook for 12 to 15 minutes, until it becomes golden brown while shaking every 6 minutes.

Lemon Tofu

Preparation time: 15 minutes

Cooking time: 25 minutes

Overall time: 40 minutes

Serves: 2 to 4 people

Recipe Ingredients:

- ❖ 1 pound of extra-firm tofu (drained and pressed)
- ❖ 1 tbsp. of tamari
- ❖ 1 tbsp. of cornstarch, or arrowroot powder

For the sauce:

- ❖ 1 tsp. of lemon zest
- ❖ 1/3 cup of lemon juice
- ❖ ½ cup of water
- ❖ 2 tbsp. of organic sugar
- ❖ 2 tsp. of cornstarch, or arrowroot powder

Cooking Instructions:

1. Cut the tofu in cubes, place the tofu cubes in a quart-size plastic storage bag and add the tamari and seal the bag.

2. Shake the bag until all the tofu is coated with the tamari. Then add the 2 tablespoons of cornstarch to the bag and shake again until the tofu is coated.

3. Set the tofu aside to preserve for at least 15 minutes. Meanwhile add all the sauce ingredients to a small bowl and mix with a spoon and set aside.

4. Place the tofu in the Air-fryer in a single layer; you will perhaps need to do this in two batches. Cook the tofu at 390°F for 10 minutes, shaking it after 5 minutes.

5. After you're done cooking the batches of tofu, add it all to a skillet over medium-high heat.

6. Stir the sauce and pour it over the tofu. Stir the tofu and sauce until the sauce is thickened and the tofu is heated through. Serve immediately with rice and steamed vegetables if desired and enjoy.

Air-Fried Spicy Cauliflower

Preparation time: 5 minutes

Cooking time: 25 minutes

Overall time: 30 minutes

Serves: 2 to 4 people

Recipe Ingredients:

- ❖ 1 head of cauliflower cut into florets
- ❖ ¾ cup of thinly sliced white onion
- ❖ 5 cloves of finely sliced garlic
- ❖ 1 ½ tbsp. of tamari or gluten free tamari
- ❖ 1 tbsp. of rice vinegar
- ❖ ½ tsp. of coconut sugar
- ❖ 1 tbsp. of Sriracha or other favorite hot sauce
- ❖ 2 scallions for garnish

Cooking Instructions:

1. Place cauliflower in your Air-fryer. If your Air-fryer is one that has holes in the bottom you'll need to use an air fryer insert.

2. Set the temperature at 350°F and cook for about 10 minutes. Open the Air-fryer, grab the pot by the handle, remove and shake and slide back in the compartment.

3. Add the sliced onion, stir and cook for 10 more minutes. After 10 minutes, add garlic, stir and cook 5 more minutes.

4. Mix soy sauce, rice vinegar, coconut sugar, Sriracha, salt and pepper together in a small bowl.

5. Add the mixture to cauliflower, stir and cook for 5 more minutes. The insert keeps all of the juices inside.

6. To serve sprinkle sliced scallions over the top for garnish and enjoy.

DESSERT RECIPES

Cinnamon Rolls

Preparation time: 5 minutes

Cooking time: 25 minutes

Overall time: 30 minutes

Recipe Ingredients:

For the rolls

- 2 tablespoons of melted butter, plus more for brushing
- 1/3 cup of packed brown sugar
- ½ teaspoon of ground cinnamon
- Kosher salt
- All-purpose flour, for surface
- 8 ounces of tube refrigerated crescent rolls

For the glaze

- 2 ounces of cream cheese, softened
- ½ cup of powdered sugar
- 1 tablespoon of whole milk, plus more if needed

Cooking Instructions:

1. To make the rolls, line the bottom of Air-fryer with parchment paper and brush with butter.

2. In a medium bowl, combine butter, brown sugar, cinnamon, and a large pinch of salt until it becomes smooth and fluffy.

3. On a lightly floured surface, roll out crescent rolls in one piece, then pinch seams together and fold in half.

4. Roll into a 9"-x-7" rectangle shape and spread butter mixture over dough, leaving ¼-inch border.

5. Beginning at a long edge, roll up dough like a jelly roll, then cut crosswise into 6 pieces.

6. Arrange pieces in prepared Air-fryer, cut-side up, spaced evenly, then set Air-fryer to 350°F and cook for 10 minutes until it becomes golden and cooked through.

7. To make the glaze, whisk cream cheese, powdered sugar, and milk together in a medium bowl and add more teaspoonful of milk if required to thin glaze. Spread glaze over warm cinnamon rolls and serve.

French Toast Sticks

Preparation time: 5 minutes

Cooking time: 30 minutes

Total Time: 35 minutes

Serves: 5 to 6 people

Recipe Ingredients:

- ❖ 2 large eggs
- ❖ 1/3 cup heavy cream
- ❖ 1/3 cup whole milk
- ❖ 3 tablespoons of granulated sugar
- ❖ ¼ teaspoon of ground cinnamon
- ❖ ½ teaspoon of pure vanilla extract
- ❖ Kosher salt
- ❖ 6 thick slices of pull man (or brioche, each slice cut into thirds)
- ❖ Maple syrup, for serving

Cooking Instructions:

1. Beat eggs, cream, milk, sugar, cinnamon, vanilla, and a pinch of salt in a large shallow baking dish, then add bread and turn to coat a few times.

2. Arrange French toast in basket of Air-fryer, working in batches as necessary to not overcrowd basket.

3. Set Air-fryer at 375°F and cook for about 8 minutes until it turns golden tossing halfway through.

4. Drizzled with maple syrup and serve toast warm!

Air Baked Molten Lava Cakes

Preparation time: 5 minutes

Cooking time: 15 minutes

Overall time: 20 minutes

Recipe Ingredients:

- ❖ 1.5 tablespoons of self-rising flour
- ❖ 3.5 tablespoons of baker's sugar
- ❖ 3.5 ounces of unsalted butter
- ❖ 3.5 ounces of dark chocolate
- ❖ 2 Eggs

Recipe Instructions:

1. Preheat your Air-fryer to 375ºF, grease and flour 4 standard oven safe ramekins.

2. Melt dark chocolate and butter in a microwave safe bowl on level 7 for 3 minutes, and stir thoroughly.

3. Remove from microwave and stir until it becomes even and consistent. Whisk the eggs and sugar until pale and frothy.

4. Pour melted chocolate mixture into egg mixture. Stir in flour then use a spatula to combine everything uniformly.

5. Fill the ramekins about ¾ full with cake mixture and bake in preheated air fryer at 375ºF for 10 minutes.

6. Remove from the Air-fryer and allow it to cool in ramekin for 2 minutes. Carefully turn ramekins upside down onto serving plate, tapping the bottom with a butter knife to loosen edges.

7. Cake should release from ramekin with little effort and center should appear dark or gooey. Serve enjoy warm with a-la-mode.

Crustless Cheesecake

Preparation time: 5 minutes

Cooking time: 10 minutes

Overall time: 15 minutes

Serves: 2 people

Recipe Ingredients:

- ❖ 16 ounces of cream cheese softened to room temperature
- ❖ ¾ cup of zero calorie sweetener (make sure it measures the same as sugar)
- ❖ 2 eggs
- ❖ 1 teaspoon of vanilla extract
- ❖ ½ teaspoon of lemon juice
- ❖ 2 tablespoons of sour cream

Cooking Instructions:

1. Preheat your Air-fryer at 350°F. In a blender, mix together the eggs, sweetener, vanilla, and lemon juice until smooth.

2. Add in the sour cream and cream cheese, blend until it becomes lump free and silky. The more you whip it, the creamier becomes.

3. Pour batter into two 4-inch spring-form pans and cook for about 8 to 10 minutes or until set.

4. Allow to cool completely in the spring-form pan. Then refrigerator overnight, or for at least for 2 to 3 hours.

5. Serve and enjoy!

Vegan Beignets with an Oven Option

Preparation time: 30 minutes

Cooking time: 6 minutes

Extra time: 1 hour 30 minutes

Overall time: 2 hours 6 minutes

Serves: 24 beignets

Recipe Ingredients:

For powdered baking blend:

- ❖ 1 cup whole earth sweetener baking blend
- ❖ 1 teaspoon organic corn starch

For the proofing:

- ❖ 1 cup full-fat coconut milk from a can
- ❖ 3 tablespoons powdered baking blend
- ❖ 1 1/2 teaspoons active baking yeast

For the dough:

- ❖ 2 tablespoons melted coconut oil
- ❖ 2 tablespoons aquafaba, the drained water from a can of chickpeas
- ❖ 2 teaspoons vanilla
- ❖ 3 cups unbleached white flour, with a little extra to sprinkle on the cutting board for later

Cooking Instructions

1. Add the whole earth baking blend and corn starch to your blender and blend until powdery smooth.

2. The cornstarch will keep it from clumping so you can store it if you don't use it all in the recipe.

3. Heat the coconut milk until it's warm but cool enough that you can stick your finger in it without burning yourself. If it's too hot, you will kill the yeast.

4. Add it to your mixer with the sugar and yeast. Let sit for about 10 minutes, until the yeast begins to foam.

5. Using the paddle attachment, mix in the coconut oil, aquafaba, and vanilla. Then add the flour a cup at a time.

6. Once the flour is mixing in and the dough is coming away from the sides of the mixer, change to your dough hook if you have one.

7. Knead the dough in your mixer for about 3 minutes. The dough will be wetter than if you were making a loaf of bread, but you should be able to scrape out the dough and form a ball without it staying on your hands.

8. Place dough in a mixing bowl and cover it with a clean dish towel and let rise for 1 hour.

9. Now sprinkle some flour over a large cutting board and pat out the dough into a rectangle that is about ⅓ inch thick.

10. After that, cut it into 24 squares and let it proof for 30 minutes before you cook them.

11. Preheat your air fryer to 390°F. Now depending on the size of your air fryer you can put 3 to 6 beignets in at a time.

12. Cook for 3 minutes on one side and flip them, then cook for another 2 minutes or until it turns golden brown.

13. Sprinkle copiously with the powdered baking blend you made in the beginning and enjoy!

Blueberry Hand Pies

Preparation time: 15 minutes

Cooking time: 12 minutes

Overall time: 27 minutes

Serves: 8 people

Recipe Ingredients:

- ❖ 1 cup of blueberries
- ❖ 2.5 tablespoons of caster sugar
- ❖ 1 teaspoon of lemon juice
- ❖ 1 Pinch of salt
- ❖ 14 oz. of refrigerated pie crust
- ❖ Water
- ❖ Vanilla sugar to sprinkle on top (optional)

Cooking Instructions:

1. In a medium bowl, mix together the blueberries, sugar, lemon juice, and salt.

2. Roll out the piecrusts (or short crust pastry roll) and cut out 6 to 8 about 4-inch individual circles.

3. Place about 1 tablespoon of the blueberry filling in the center of each circle.

4. Moisten edges of dough with water, and fold the dough over the filling to form a half moon shape.

5. With a fork, gently crimp the edges of the piecrust together. Then cut three slits on the top of the hand pies.

6. Spray the hand pies with cooking spray and sprinkle with vanilla sugar if you are using it.

7. Then preheat your Air-fryer to 350°F. Place 3 to 4 hand pies in single layer inside the Air-fryer basket and cook for about 9 to 12 minutes, or until it turns golden brown.

8. Let the pies cool for at least 10 minutes before serving.

Air-Fried Spiced Apples

Preparation time: 5 minutes

Cooking time: 10 minutes

Overall time: 15 minutes

Serves: 2 to 4 people

Recipe Ingredients:

- ❖ 4 small sliced apples
- ❖ 2 tbsp. of ghee or coconut oil, melted
- ❖ 2 tbsp. of sugar
- ❖ 1 tsp. of apple pie spice

Cooking Instructions:

1. Place the apples in a bowl and drizzle with ghee or coconut oil. Sprinkle again with sugar and apple pie spice and stir thoroughly coat the apples.

2. Place the apples in a small pan that is made for Air-fryers and then place that inside the basket.

3. Set the Air-fryer at 350°F for 10 minutes, and then pierce the apples with a fork to ensure they are tender.

4. If needed place back in Air-fryer for an additional 3 to 5 minutes.

5. Serve with ice cream or whipped topping.

Chocolate Chip Cookie

Preparation time: 15 minutes

Cooking time: 10 minutes

Overall time: 25 minutes

Serves: 2 to 8

Recipe Ingredients:

- ½ cup of butter softened
- ½ cup of sugar
- ½ cup of light brown sugar
- 1 egg
- 1 teaspoon of vanilla
- ½ teaspoon of baking soda
- ¼ teaspoon of salt
- 1 ½ cups of all-purpose flour
- 1 cup of chocolate chips or chocolate chunks

Cooking Instructions:

1. Preheat your Air-fryer to 350°F, and then grease two glass or metal pans that will fit in your Air-fryer.

2. Cream together butter, sugar, brown sugar and add egg and vanilla. Now mix in baking soda, salt, and flour, stir thoroughly in a chocolate chips/chucks.

3. Press cookie dough into bottom of greased pan one after the other and bake 10 to 12 minutes until it is lightly browned around the edges.

4. Serve immediately and enjoy!

Cherry Pies

Preparation time: 5 minutes

Cooking time: 10 minutes

Overall time: 15 minutes

Serves: 6 people

Recipe Ingredients:

For pies:

- ❖ 14 ounces of package refrigerated pie crusts
- ❖ ½ cup cherry pie filling
- ❖ Non-stick cooking spray

For glaze:

- ❖ 3 tablespoons of confectioner's sugar
- ❖ ½ teaspoon milk

Cooking Instructions:

1. Firstly, unroll the refrigerated pie crusts according to package directions.

2. Cut out 6 pies with cookie cutter and place 1.5 tablespoons of cherry pie filling near the center of each piece of dough.

3. Fold pie in half and seal edge by pressing lightly with tines of a fork. Make 3 small cuts in top of dough.

4. After that, place into the basket of Air-fryer and spray lightly with non-stick cooking spray.

5. Cook in Air-fryer for approximately 10 minutes at 350°F. After 10 minutes, remove when lightly browned and allow it to cool.

6. Mix glaze ingredients thoroughly to remove lumps, after that, drizzle over top of cooled pies. Serve and enjoy!

Cheesecake Egg Rolls

Preparation time: 15 minutes

Cooking time: 17 minutes

Overall time: 32 minutes

Serves: 15 rolls

Recipe Ingredients:

- ❖ 16 oz. (2 packages) of cream cheese, at room temperature
- ❖ ½ cup of (100g) granulated sugar
- ❖ 1 tbsp. of lemon juice
- ❖ 1 tsp. of vanilla extract
- ❖ 8.5 oz. (1 jar) fig jam
- ❖ 15 refrigerated ready-made egg roll wrappers
- ❖ Egg wash: 1 egg beaten with 1 tbsp. of water
- ❖ Olive oil cooking spray
- ❖ 2 tbsp. of unsalted butter, melted
- ❖ ¼ cup of sugar
- ❖ 1 tsp. of ground cinnamon

Cooking Instructions:

1. In the bowl of an electric mixer fitted with the whip attachment, combine the cream cheese, sugar, lemon juice and vanilla extract.

2. Mix thoroughly on medium speed for 2 minutes to combine. Then remove cheesecake filling to a pastry bag or to a zip top bag with a corner snipped.

3. Stir the jam well in its jar so that it loosens and can easily be scooped with a spoon.

4. Lay an egg roll wrapper with a pointed end toward you; in the center, pipe on approximately 2 tablespoons cream cheese mixture.

5. Top with one tablespoon of jam and then use a pastry brush to coat the edges of the egg roll wrapper with egg wash.

6. Fold bottom corner over filling, roll snugly half-way to cover filling. Fold in both sides snugly against the filling.

7. Roll wrap up, making sure the top corner is well-sealed with the egg wash. Spray egg rolls with olive oil cooking spray on both sides.

8. Preheat Air-fryer to 370°F for 10 minutes allowing the egg rolls to stand at room temperature while the fryer heats.

9. Place 4 to 5 egg rolls in the hot fryer basket and fry for 5 to 7 minutes, or until the egg rolls are golden brown on top.

10. Just like regular frying, you can count on at least one egg roll breaking and releasing filling during cooking.

11. Clean up using a paper towel to wipe out the basket (be careful if it's still hot!). Remove rolls from the basket and let it cool. Repeat frying until all of the egg rolls are cooked.

12. Now lightly brush golden tops of egg rolls with melted butter, and then combine sugar and cinnamon in a small bowl and sprinkle over egg rolls.

13. Serve warm or at room temperature and store leftovers in the refrigerator.

Acknowledgement

In preparing the "Ultimate Air Fryer Cookbook for Beginners", I sincerely wish to acknowledge my indebtedness to my husband for his support and the wholehearted cooperation and vast experience of my two colleagues - Mrs. Barbara Miles, and Mrs. Alexander Bedria.

PATRICIA WEISS

Printed in the USA
CPSIA information can be obtained
at www.ICGtesting.com
CBHW080528240724
12047CB00019B/602